101 WAYS TO REDUCE YOUR CARBON FOOTPRINT

101 WAYS TO REDUCE YOUR CARBON FOOTPRINT

Simple Things You Can Do to Lessen Your Impact on the Environment

ANDREA BOHMHOLDT

Silverleaf Press Books are available exclusively
through Independent Publishers Group.

For details, write or telephone:
Independent Publishers Group
814 North Franklin St.
Chicago, IL 60610
(312) 337-0747

Silverleaf Press
4110 South Highland Drive, Suite 300
Salt Lake City, Utah 84124

ISBN-13: 978-1-93439-334-5

This book is dedicated to my family.

CONTENTS

*We do not inherit the earth
from our ancestors. We
borrow it from our children.*

Native American Proverb

FOREWORD

In 2001, I was teaching high school media literacy and film and video production. As a science writer and journalist, I was not a stranger to the science and politics of global warming. On the day the National Academy reported back to President George W. Bush that the science behind the third assessment of the Intergovernmental Panel on Climate Change was good science, I told my classes that there would be all kinds of news stories over the span of their lives, but that global warming would be the really big news from that day on. Guess what? I was wrong.

Sometimes the things that should be the top stories just aren't. As one editor facetiously asked me when I pitched a story about a community's response to the threat of global warming, "Oh, is it still warming?"

Like, it's not hot yet, so what do we care?

So why do so many people resist the relatively simple concept that the energy use and farming and forestry practices of several billion people are affecting our atmosphere—especially when fixing it would help our and the planet's other species a great deal? At face value, this should be a no-brainer.

In 1988, I posed a solution to a friend, an environmentalist then in his nineties who had known Rachel Carson: Why don't we start banning cars from certain roads at particular times of the day, some days of the week? We'd force people to take public transportation! "What public transportation?" he asked with a chuckle. "You can't expect people to change when you haven't given them something to change to."

The answer to our current dilemma is the same answer I received two decades earlier: People aren't taking action to do something about global warming because they feel powerless. All the talk about "dangerous climate change" is making them cover their ears. We have to offer solutions.

During a conference call to discuss leveraging an IPCC report to promote action on a piece of federal legislation—a call that involved a cadre of folks in Washington and New York, and various others of us scattered about the U.S.—a voice from the hinterlands

asked through the static, "What about the solutions? Shouldn't we talk about the solutions?" Came the response from someone inside the Beltway: "Oh, that's the Carper bill."

But bills and wonderful ideas like deserts full of solar cells and algae, while they make great goals and terrific targets, lack a crucial ingredient: We can't do them. We—the people who have to keep our heads out of the sand; who have to listen to the tales of feedback loops, floods, droughts, starvation, and war; who have to stay in this in order to get Congressional delegations to pass a climate bill and governors to allow off-shore wind and state legislatures to pass renewable energy incentives—we need things we can do. They need to be simple, easy, inexpensive, normal, unweird things. They should not look as funny or cost anywhere near as much as an Insight or a Prius, a photovoltaic array or a windmill. We need to be able to just do them.

The genius of this book, written by my friend Andrea Bohmholdt, is that these 101 things are just like that—you can do them. And you can do most of them right now. So stop reading this and get to it. We are running out of time!

Bill Burtis, Manager of Communications and Special Projects
Clean Air–Cool Planet

If we do not change our direction, we are likely to end up where we are headed.

Chinese Proverb

INTRODUCTION

If you're reading this book, you've made a decision to be part of the solution to climate change. Although you are only one person, you have an impact on the environment and can make a difference in the world. This book can be a useful tool for gathering information and forming new habits that conserve energy, save money, and reduce your individual impact on the climate.

Although we don't know how violently the effects of climate change will impact the earth and humanity, we do know that human activities are causing dramatic increases of greenhouse gases (GHGs), which are changing our climate. Climate change can cause more frequent extreme weather events, similar to Hurricane Katrina, which hit the United States in 2005. We could also lose to extinction more than one-third of the plant and animal species on the planet. Some areas may experience an increase in the intensity of droughts, while coastal areas may encounter increased flooding from the rising sea level. The changing climate can also affect agricultural production, decreasing world food supplies. We are all interconnected, and climate change has the potential to affect everything on this planet.

You may have heard about climate change but wondered what you can do to make a difference. Actually, there is a lot you can do! There are many small steps you can take to significantly reduce your individual impact on the planet. Forming new habits and changing your routine takes practice, but this can be easily accomplished just one day at a time. Conserving energy not only reduces your carbon footprint, it also translates into saving money—a motivating factor—and can be realized immediately.

This book makes suggestions on reducing your carbon footprint that can easily be incorporated into your everyday life. None of us is perfect, but we can focus on making at least one improvement every day, which can lead to daily habits and lifestyle changes. Not all of us can build an energy-efficient house or lead a completely sustainable life, but all of us have room for improvement. Indeed, as a nation, Americans tend to consume more energy per person than do residents of any other country. As Americans, we want to be the leaders of progress, not foot-draggers.

You may be thinking, *How do I start?* Well, first assess your impact on the environment by calculating your carbon footprint. A personal carbon footprint is a measure of your impact on the environment, specifically greenhouse gas emissions that result from your activities and that contribute to climate change. Although it is difficult to quantify a personal carbon footprint with complete accuracy, using a carbon calculator can give you a good estimate of the greenhouse gas emissions caused by your actions. There are many carbon calculators available online. You may want to compare your results from two or three different carbon calculators to get a good idea of your impact. The carbon calculators vary from very simple to complex, and you will probably need your utility bills to get started. You can search for a calculator by typing "carbon calculator" into a search engine on the Internet. Some useful calculators include:

www.carbonfootprint.com/calculator.aspx

http://www.nature.org/initiatives/climatechange/calculator/

http://epa.gov/climatechange/emissions/ind_calculator.html

http://www.safeclimate.net/calculator/

Once you have calculated your carbon footprint, document it and use it as a baseline number. After you have implemented the suggestions from this book, calculate your carbon footprint again. Then subtract your new carbon footprint from your baseline carbon footprint to determine the net reduction of emissions. You'll be amazed how all these minor changes add up. Calculate your carbon footprint at least every year and create targets for you and your household to work towards.

It is important to first reduce your carbon footprint as much as possible through conservation and energy efficiency, but if you would like to reduce your carbon footprint even further, offsets can help. Carbon offsets are commodities bought and sold in a voluntary market in the United States. The idea is to invest in an emissions-reduction project somewhere in the world to equivocally offset or reduce your carbon footprint. This is not as simple as it may sound, and it is important to research an organization before sending money. Some organizations are making powerful changes in our world, but others are buying acres of trees that were not actually threatened by deforestation, or planting trees in places not necessarily prime for carbon sequestration. The most important concept to consider when assessing offsets is additionality, meaning that the project to reduce the emissions would not have taken place unless it had funding from contributions like yours, and that the project reduces emissions that would not have already been reduced from "business as usual" or from regulation. For more information about selecting a carbon offsetting organization, see "A Consumer's Guide to Retail Carbon Offset Providers," available online at the Clean Air–Cool Planet website.

In addition to the resources above, *101 Ways to Reduce Your Carbon Footprint* is full of suggestions for reducing your carbon footprint. It is divided into four sections: Personal Habits, At Home, Transportation, and Community Involvement. Although there are many more ways to reduce your carbon footprint, this book covers the basics of what any person can do—without investing a lot of money. In fact, following the suggestions in this book will most likely *save* you money. The suggestions are not in any particular ranking or order and are not meant to be inclusive. I hope this book inspires you to change your habits and be part of the solution to climate change rather than part of the problem.

*We must not, in trying to think
about how we can make a big
difference, ignore the small daily
differences we can make, which,
over time, add up to big differences
that we often cannot foresee.*[1]

Marian Wright Edelman

PERSONAL HABITS

Almost every product we use involves the release of greenhouse gas. The full accounting of the emissions caused by a product is called a life-cycle analysis. The life-cycle analysis begins at the sourcing of the raw materials and tallies the emissions from manufacturing, the use of the product, and the after-life of the product (meaning how the product is disposed of and dissolved). For example, the life cycle analysis (LCA) of a cotton T-shirt would begin with determining how many greenhouse gas emissions were caused by cultivating and harvesting the cotton, then adding the emissions from the manufacturing process and the transportation of all the components used to make the T-shirt, plus the gases emitted in creating the energy used to wash and dry the

T-shirt throughout its life, and finally totaling it with what is emitted after the T-shirt finally makes it to the landfill to decompose. As you can tell, a life-cycle analysis of just one product is very extensive and expensive, although the expense of performing a LCA has not stopped many large companies from determining the life-cycle emissions caused by their products. Soon we may start comparing the carbon footprint of the products we buy in stores as we do with food labels today. Labeling products with their emissions impact helps consumers make good decisions and also promotes buying local products over products that have been imported from the other side of the world.

The greatest gift we have is the ability to make personal choices. Those small decisions that fill every day of our lives can make a tremendous impact on our planet. Hopefully, the upcoming sections will give you some new ideas or reinforce good habits you already have. It's easy to form good habits if you just focus on making one small change each day. Put this book on your nightstand or next to your favorite recliner. Every morning, start your day off with one change to make the world a better place. Use this book as a reference to keep you on track. Soon (if you don't already) you'll probably have a voice in the back of your head reminding you to reduce, reuse, and recycle.

I am only one,
But still I am one.
I cannot do everything,
But still I can do something:
And because I cannot do everything,
I will not refuse to do the
something that I can do. [2]

Edward Everett Hale

The Little Things

1. BRING YOUR OWN CUP

If you're like me, you need a cup of coffee, tea, or hot chocolate to get you up and going in the morning—or maybe several cups. So when you stop by the coffee shop on your way to work, take your own refillable mug or thermos. With your own container, you'll probably pay less for a cup of hot beverage, but more importantly, you won't need a disposable cup, cardboard sleeve, and plastic lid. If you normally buy a cup of coffee, tea, or hot chocolate every day, that's 365 fewer cups, cardboard sleeves, and lids in the landfill every year! If you forget your refillable mug, take the time to enjoy your fresh brew in a washable mug provided by the coffee shop. You might try leaving your reusable mug or thermos (or a spare) in your car. You can also keep a reusable coffee mug at your desk at work and another one at home. It's better to have three mugs you can wash and reuse than to waste numerous disposable cups. If you don't drink hot drinks, the same concept applies to other beverages. Instead of buying a plastic bottle or plastic cup, bring your own reusable container and refill it at the store or drinking fountain.

If you already bring your own coffee mug on a daily basis, encourage others to do so. Using an extra coffee mug, bring some coffee to a friend or colleague who uses a lot of disposable cups. Tell him or her how much money you save by refilling your coffee mug and how much waste you avoid. To calculate the annual amount of waste you create by using disposable coffee cups, visit the coffee waste calculator at http://www.dzignism.com/projects/coffee.waste/.

When you use your own coffee mug or other reusable container, you avoid waste, save energy, and reduce your carbon footprint. Over time, you might also save a significant amount of money.

2. USE REUSABLE CANVAS BAGS

Since plastic bags are so cheap to produce, we tend to overuse them. You may think paper bags are a better option, but it actually takes more energy and causes more pollution to produce a paper bag than a plastic bag. It also takes more energy to recycle a paper bag, but only a small fraction of plastic bags actually get recycled. The plastic bags that become litter or end up in a landfill can take about five hundred years to break down. Also, the plastic bag may have traveled from Asia, therefore causing more emissions from transportation.

Indeed, there is quite a debate about which choice is better, paper or plastic, but there is a solution. Next time you go to the grocery store and the checker asks, "Paper or plastic?" say, "Neither!" Instead, bring your own reusable canvas or heavy-duty bags. You'd be amazed how efficient and sturdy these bags are. You can pack a lot more groceries into one bag, and you don't have to worry about the bag ripping and sending your food all over the parking lot. If you place the bags on your food in the checkout line, the bagger will pack your groceries in the canvas bags, and some stores offer a discount when you bring your own bags.

A pet peeve of mine is watching a checker bag something very small, like a pack of gum, or use a different bag for each item. If you're only buying a few items, you probably don't even need a bag at all, but you'll have to tell the checker immediately if you don't want one, or your items will be bagged before you know it.

Using canvas bags also makes it easier to bring your groceries into your house once you arrive home. Instead of trying to bring twenty plastic bags into the house, you may only have to carry a few canvas bags. The only problem is remembering to bring the canvas bags with you to the grocery store. I've gotten into the habit of leaving the bags next to my keys after I shop,

so that the next time I need to use my car, I take the bags with me and leave them in my car. That way, the next time I'm at the grocery store, I only have to walk back to my car if I forget them.

3. USE RECHARGEABLE BATTERIES

Batteries are used to power many of the items we use daily. If you aren't using rechargeable batteries, it's like throwing money and energy in the landfill, not to mention toxic heavy metals and chemicals such as mercury, lead, cadmium, silver, and chromium. Currently, the best solution is to use rechargeable nickel metal hydride (NiMH) batteries, which contain no toxic heavy metals. You can use NiMH batteries numerous times before they need to be replaced. Unlike other batteries, you don't have to dispose of them like hazardous waste or have them shipped to Japan or Switzerland to be recycled. Imagine all the fossil fuels burned just to ship used batteries clear across the world to be recycled.

Using a rapid charger saves energy by charging your batteries in one to two hours, and does not deplete the life of the rechargeable battery. In fact, using a charger that needs twelve hours to charge batteries is more likely to reduce the life of the battery than a quick charger. Be sure to unplug the charger as soon as the batteries are fully charged; otherwise the charger will continue using power, thereby eliminating the advantage and energy savings of the quick charge.

To get the most out of your rechargeable batteries, use the battery until it is completely depleted and only charge it if you plan to use it soon. To retain the energy of NiMH batteries, store them in your freezer, but let them warm to room temperature before using them. To conserve more energy, limit the number of items you use that need batteries.

4. TURN THE LIGHTS OFF

Sounds simple enough, right? But there may be lights you leave on that you don't even think about. For example, do you turn the lights off before leaving a public restroom? Obviously you don't want to turn the lights out if the restroom is occupied, but if not, shut them off before you leave. Some public restrooms have enough sunlight that electric lights are unnecessary during the day. At the workplace, you could make a small sign by the light switches requesting that others shut the lights off before they leave. You can make a habit of turning the lights off every time you leave a room. During the day, just use the natural light from the sun to light your

home and workplace. If you need to use a light, use only the necessary lights. For instance, use a lamp with one bulb to light the area you need instead of using four florescent overhead lights.

5. RECONSIDER COMPUTER AND PRINTER USE

These days, most of us can't get by without using a computer for something. You may use a computer all day long for work or school, or you may just use it occasionally. Whatever the case may be, your computer habits can affect the amount of energy you use. You can adjust the power settings on your computer so that after a certain period of inactivity, the monitor will turn off, the computer will go into standby mode, or the hard drive will shut down. If you use a laptop, you can create different energy settings depending on whether the laptop is plugged in or operating on the battery. Most computers also have a hibernation mode. In this mode, the computer is turned off, but when it is restarted any open programs and documents are restored.

You can adjust the power settings to accommodate your computer habits. If you are interrupted often when you are on the computer, you may want to set your computer to go into standby mode after five minutes of inactivity. If you tend to forget to turn off the computer, or stay away from your computer for longer periods of time, you may want to set your computer to hibernate after fifteen minutes. Also, you can set your monitor to shut down first, giving you some warning before the computer goes into standby or hibernation mode.

If you use a laptop computer, take advantage of the battery. Charge your battery only when necessary, using the battery until it is completely depleted before recharging it. Your laptop will warn you when your battery is getting low. Remember to unplug the charger after charging the battery; otherwise, the charger will continue to use power even if your computer is not plugged in. In addition, whether you use a laptop or a desktop computer, leaving your computer on all day or overnight causes unnecessary wear on computer parts and wastes energy.

Minimize printer use by sending and receiving information electronically and keeping the printer turned off unless it is being used. More and more people are relying on email for the majority of their communication needs. Email eliminates the need to print or mail information. Furthermore, most documents can be sent and received electronically. Many university professors actually prefer receiving assignments electronically rather than in paper form. Also, you can track your editing with most word-processing software, which eliminates the need to print numerous drafts. When doing research for school, remember that most articles are available electronically, eliminating the need to photocopy books. It is also much easier to keep track of articles in electronic form.

6. TAKE THE STAIRS

When I worked in an office and when I was in college, I sat at a desk for almost eight hours a day and didn't get much exercise. As a result, I didn't have much energy. Interestingly enough, the more I exercised, the more energy I had and the happier I was. Sometimes it can be difficult to get exercise during the day, but there are little things we can do to get a little exercise and save energy, like using the stairs instead of the elevator.

In college, one of my professors always used the stairs, whether he was going up one floor or six. It made me feel lazy when he passed me as I waited for the elevators—especially when he beat me to the next floor. So I started to follow his example. I realized that not only was I wasting energy (and sometimes time), I was also missing an opportunity to get a little exercise. Try taking the stairs next time. Start with one flight of stairs and increase your use of the stairs each day. You may surprise yourself!

7. REUSE TOWELS AND BED SHEETS AT HOTELS

At hotels, washing and drying towels and sheets every day uses a great deal of energy. In addition, some hotels outsource their laundry to a laundry service, which means there are added emissions caused by the transportation of the linens. You don't wash your towels and bed sheets at home every day, do you? It makes perfect sense for hotels to wash towels and bed sheets between guests, but do you really need freshly washed towels and sheets every day when you're out of town? You can save energy by requesting not to have your towels and sheets washed every day of your stay. Many hotels now encourage guest to forego daily washing of towels and sheets. You may not stay in hotels very often, but when you do, consider reducing energy use just as you would in your own home, asking personnel to hold off laundering until you've finished your stay.

8. UNPLUG YOUR CHARGERS

Do you leave your cell-phone charger plugged in even if your phone isn't attached? Did you know that cell-phone chargers draw electricity whether your cell phone is attached or not? This is also true for MP3 players, portable video games, and other portable electronic devices. Once your phone is charged, if you leave it connected to the charger and leave the charger plugged in, the electricity keeps flowing through the charger and is wasted. To avoid this inefficiency, designate an area to charge all of your portable electronic devices and charge them at the same time of day, when it is most convenient for you. That way, when they are done charging, you can unplug them instead of leaving them plugged in overnight or forgetting about them. You may consider this to be a small amount of energy, but it all adds up, especially if you've left your chargers plugged in 24/7 in the past.

9. EXAMINE YOUR EATING HABITS

Reducing your consumption of meat (including poultry)—or even better, becoming a vegetarian—can make a lasting impact on your health, the environment, and your peace of mind. Did you know that in the United States more than half of all water, one-third of fossil fuels used, and 87% of agricultural land is devoted to raising animals for food?[3] That's a lot of resources being used to produce meat, especially considering that the average person in the United States consumes more than two hundred pounds of meat and poultry per year.[4] It takes many more resources to support a meat-eating diet than a vegetarian diet. Over a lifetime, imagine the toll those extra resources can on the environment, not to mention your health. Conversely, many resources can be conserved by not eating meat or by purchasing meat less often, not to mention sparing the many animals that are being tortured every day to provide meat for humans. If you've ever wondered why some people become animal-rights activists, take a look at some videos from the PETA website at www.peta.org.

You may be surprised how easy being a vegetarian can be. I've been a vegetarian since I was fifteen years old, and I recently excluded dairy products from my diet as well. Most restaurants have vegetarian options on their menus,

and if not they will usually accommodate your request for a vegetarian meal. Only once have I ever had to leave a restaurant because there wasn't a vegetarian option available, and that was ten years ago. The selection of vegetarian foods at the typical grocery store has increased significantly in the past five years, and it is no longer necessary to go to a specialty health-food store to satisfy your daily needs.

Start simple: stop eating meat for breakfast. Your arteries and your heart will thank you. Perhaps you could carry your new habit over to lunch and stop eating meat for lunch, then plan a few dinners every week without meat. Try a vegetarian option the next time you go out to eat. Some fast-food restaurants like Burger King even offer veggie burgers. Practice eating less meat every day, and you'll be surprised that, before long, you won't even miss it.

*There is enough on the earth
for everybody's need, but
not for everyone's greed.*

Mahatma Gandhi

Purchasing Decisions

10. REDUCE WASTE

"Reduce, reuse, and recycle" is a common mantra for reducing your carbon footprint. Reducing waste means both consuming less and throwing away less. Reducing is the best way to prevent waste from the source. To reduce waste, you can compost kitchen scraps, purchase goods wisely, and even better, don't purchase non-essentials.

Composting organic waste such as kitchen scraps, grass clippings, and fallen leaves is a great way to improve the physical properties of the soil in your yard and to grow healthy plants and trees. Using mature compost as fertilizer eliminates the need for chemical fertilizers and saves money, too. For more information about composting, visit: www.compostguide.com

Waste that ends up in a landfill produces methane, a harmful greenhouse gas that causes more damage per ton than does carbon dioxide. Although it is possible to use methane as an energy source, until our infrastructure is capable of capturing all the methane from landfills and using it for energy instead of letting it escape into the atmosphere, we need to reduce waste as much as possible. And even if that time comes, we don't need to add to what's already piled on the planet.

11. REUSE

Reusing goods is better than recycling. It is better to buy and use products that are durable and reusable than disposable goods. If you no longer need a product, you could sell it or donate it to charity or a local thrift store. Automobiles, cell phones, and computers can be donated to local charities. Conversely, instead of buying something new, you could purchase something used from your local thrift store or repair something instead of throwing it away.

My favorite place to shop is the thrift store. You'd be amazed what you can find. I've purchased name-brand clothes, recreational gear, furniture, kitchen items, and tools for the yard. The list goes on and on. Before you go to the store to purchase a new item, check the thrift store first. When you go to the thrift store, bring a bag of clothes or other household items to donate. Donations are tax deductible, so make sure you get a receipt. You'll never feel guilty about buying something from the thrift store, because if you don't need whatever you purchased, you can just donate it again. I go through my home at least once a month, looking for items I don't use. If I haven't used it in the past year, I donate it to charity or a local thrift store. Donating will make you more aware of your needs versus your wants, so you won't buy unnecessary items in the future.

12. RECYCLE

If you've reduced waste and started reusing items but still have waste, make sure you recycle what you can. Most cities have curbside recycling pickup along with the garbage, but if yours doesn't, find your local recycling drop-off station. Most curbside recycling programs will recycle aluminum, cardboard, and paper (not all types, though), plastic, and steel. (Often that doesn't include the wrappers or ink-stained packaging.) Be sure you wash recyclable products if they contained food, since products cannot be recycled if they have food in them. If you don't properly prepare products, or if you mix in types that aren't recyclable in your area, the whole lot is often thrown out. So get educated about what your city does and doesn't recycle.

You can also recycle batteries, used motor oil, used oil filters, paint, printer ink cartridges, cell phones, computers, appliances that cannot be fixed, and automobiles, but you must take them to the appropriate recycling centers. You can find the nearest battery recycling center by visiting rbrc.com online or by calling 1-800-8-BATTERY. If you like to change your own motor oil, you can recycle the used oil at most places that perform oil changes, free of charge. Recycling reduces your carbon footprint because recycled materials use less energy and generate less pollution than sourcing new products from raw materials. (To learn about what types of items and their packaging can or can't be recycled, check out the following website: http://www.obviously.com/recycle/guides/common.html.)

13. BUY RECYCLED PAPER AND OTHER PRODUCTS

Besides recycling your own product waste, it is also very important to purchase items that contain recycled materials rather than similar, non-recycled products. When purchasing products that contain recycled materials, it is important to identify

if the recycled matter is pre-consumer or post-consumer. Post-consumer recycled materials are preferred since they come from end products that have been recycled by consumers. The higher the percentage of post-consumer recycled materials in a product, the better. By purchasing recycled products, you are promoting recycling and prompting manufacturers to incorporate recycled materials into their products.

When purchasing recycled paper, it is also important to identify if the paper is FSC certified and if chlorine or chlorine derivatives were used in the processing of the paper. Forest Stewardship Council or FSC certification means that the trees harvested to make the paper meet the forest management standards of FSC. Processed Chlorine Free (PCF), Totally Chlorine Free (TCF), and Elemental Chlorine Free (ECF) identify paper that was produced without adding chlorine or chlorine derivatives during the bleaching process. Using chlorine and chlorine derivatives in the processing of paper creates toxic pollutants. For more information, visit Papercalculator.org

14. DON'T BUY PLASTIC WATER BOTTLES

According to the Natural Resources Defense Council (NRDC), "More than half of all Americans drink bottled water; about a third of the public consumes it regularly." And according to the Container Recycling Institute, 80% of disposable water bottles end up in landfills.[5] That's a lot of plastic water bottles that, if incinerated, release greenhouse gases. According to the Beverage Marketing Corporation, 185 million gallons of bottled water were imported to the United

States in 2006.[6] That means a massive amount of fossil fuels was burned just to transport your bottle of water.

Many people think that bottled water is safer than water from your kitchen tap, but that is not always the case. Coca-Cola and Pepsi actually distribute bottled tap water.[7] Bottling companies do not have to meet any regulations for water quality. Therefore, bottled-water quality may actually be worse than or no different from that of tap water.

So why do people buy plastic bottles of water? Many enjoy the convenience and are simply uninformed as to the money they are wasting and the harm they are causing to the environment. Make a statement by carting around your own reusable water bottle and refilling it as necessary. If you are concerned about the quality of your tap water, you can use an additional filter on your tap or filter the water separately using a water filtration system. In addition, there are sturdy water bottles that come equipped with filters in the cap. If you still prefer bottled water, you can purchase durable five-gallon water jugs that are refillable and reusable. Most grocery stores have a station for refilling water jugs, or there are specialty stores that only sell water. If you must purchase water in plastic bottles, make sure you recycle the bottle, even if it may be inconvenient.

15. BUY LOCALLY

Buying locally means buying goods and services produced or grown as close to your home as possible in order to minimize transportation. A tremendous amount of fossil fuels are burned to transport food and other goods to consumers. Also, most fresh food has to be refrigerated to keep it from spoiling while it is being transported, which uses even more energy. The number of miles driven to stock a grocery store

can be up to twenty-seven times higher than the amount of miles traveled by goods available through local sources.[8] In the United States, the average grocery store's produce travels nearly 1,500 miles from where it was grown to your refrigerator.[9] However, food purchased locally may only need to travel fifty miles or less.

When you purchase food that was produced locally, you get fresher food, and you help support your local economy. The money you spend locally is recirculated back into your local economy, supporting new jobs and sustaining the existing jobs. Farmers markets are a great place to find locally grown and produced goods, and you can be sure that most of the money spent will help support small farmers. Farmers markets are also a great place to ask questions about how the food was grown. If you live near a metropolitan area, there is probably a farmers market nearby. To find the farmers market near you, check out the following webpage on the Internet: http://www.ams.usda.gov/farmersmarkets.

Extend local buying beyond the farmers market to all your purchases, where possible. Check where products come from. For example, buy wine from the closest area instead of from across the world. Check the labels on clothes and try to purchase items made close to home. This can be difficult, especially when more and more items are imported from China and fewer items are being made in the United States—even more reason to support local production of goods and services.

16. EAT FRUITS AND VEGETABLES IN SEASON

How far did your fruits and vegetables have to travel before making it to your kitchen? Know what fruits and vegetables are grown locally and when they are in season. Most fruit has a label identifying where it was grown. Buy fruits and vegetables in bulk when they are in season, then can or dry them. If you can grow fruits and vegetables in your own yard, you can save money and enjoy delicious, fresh food that is free of pesticides and preservatives. There's a big difference in taste between fresh, organic produce and fruits and vegetables that were picked early and transported 1500 miles or more to your local grocery store. Some people have begun eating only foods grown within one hundred miles of their home and calling it the one-hundred-mile diet. If you would like to learn more about the 100-mile diet, visit http://100milediet.org/home. To find out when fruits and vegetables are in season in your area, visit http://www.sustainabletable.org/shop/eatseasonal/.

17. PURCHASE ENERGY-EFFICIENT PRODUCTS

When making purchasing decisions, it is imperative to assess the energy efficiency of the product, especially large appliances. If possible, purchase electronics (other than computers) that do not have a standby mode, to ensure that when they're off, they aren't using electricity. Take note if the product features the Energy Star label. Energy Star is a government program designed to identify appliances that meet strict energy-efficiency standards set by the Environmental Protection Agency (EPA) and the U.S. Department of Energy. The website Energystar.gov provides useful information about household products that meet the Energy Star standards. Even if you pay a little more for an energy-efficient product, you will recoup the difference and then some by the reduction in your utility bill over the lifetime use of the product.

18. DOWNLOAD MEDIA AND SOFTWARE

The internet is a readily accessible and valuable resource. If you do not have internet access at home, you can use the internet at your local library. In addition, most coffee shops offer free wireless internet access for patrons. Instead of purchasing physical products, you can download many products from the internet. For instance, you can download software online instead of buying the CD (and the packaging) from the store. You can also download music and watch movies online, even download and read articles instead of printing them. Sometimes it is even less expensive to purchase and download products online than from a retail store. We live in the electronic age, and just about any information you need is accessible through the internet. If you are intimidated by the internet, consider taking a computer class through a community program or from a local college.

19. AVOID PRODUCTS WITH EXCESS PACKAGING MATERIALS

The largest source of waste at most retail stores is in packaging materials. When making a purchasing decision, consider the packaging of the product and ask yourself: "Is it made with recycled materials? Can the packaging be recycled? Is there more packaging material than necessary? Can the packaging be recycled or reused?" Make selections based upon which products meet your criteria.

If you do purchase a product or receive a package that contains polystyrene loose fill, known as "peanuts" and used for packaging, locate a shipping company that can reuse them. The Plastic Loose Fill Council has a website to facilitate the reuse of "peanuts" anywhere in the country. You can search the council's database for the nearest drop-off location. Visit the webpage at LooseFillPackaging.com or call the hotline, 1-800-828-2214.

Some products are available in concentrated form, which reduces the amount of packaging without reducing the quality, and which sometimes reduces the cost per use. Another way to help conserve packaging materials is to buy in bulk. Instead of buying products that are individually packaged per serving size, buy a larger amount of the same product. By buying a larger quantity of something you know you will consume, you save money and reduce waste. If you live alone or don't think your household will be able to consume bulk foods before they expire, perhaps you can split the food and the cost with a neighbor, friend, or extended family member.

20. ELIMINATE JUNK MAIL

Have you ever asked a neighbor or friend to collect your mail for you when you've gone away on vacation? Isn't it a bit overwhelming when you return to a huge stack of paper, the majority of which you don't want or need? To save paper and trees, you can pay your bills online and receive electronic statements instead of receiving a paper statement and mailing a check. If you do need to print a statement for some reason, they will be easier to manage online, since you don't need to track them down somewhere in the house.

To avoid receiving junk mail, do not to sign up for mailing lists. Many times companies will lure you into a mailing list by disguising it as an entry form for a contest. If you currently receive catalogs, call the company and ask to be removed from their mailing list. You can usually view the catalog online instead. If you've already subscribed to magazines, donate the old ones to libraries, hospitals, or senior centers. Usually not much paper from magazines and catalogs can be recycled, because the paper is oversaturated with ink. A good option is to subscribe to magazines electronically or visit your local library for a current issue. If you'd like to receive less junk mail, you can remove your name from Direct Marketing Association lists by visiting DMAConsumers.org and clicking on "Remove my name from those lists" on the left

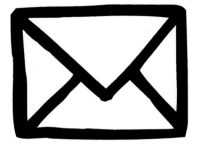

side of the web page. I've done this and have noticed a difference in the amount of mail I receive. I'm down to receiving only a couple of pieces of mail each week instead of an unmanageable stack.

21. USE THE USPS FOR SHIPPING

Sometimes you can't send or receive something electronically and must use a shipping service. If you have the option of picking the shipping method, choose the U.S. Postal Service (USPS). Their rates are competitive with other shipping companies, plus in some areas they deliver mail mostly on foot. The USPS delivers to your home or neighborhood daily (except Sundays and holidays), whereas other shipping services must make a special trip to your neighborhood to deliver a package.

The USPS is conscious of its impact on the environment and the climate. All express mail and priority mail packaging (free to the public) meet "Cradle to Cradle" SM Silver certification. To achieve the certification, all of the two hundred suppliers that contribute to producing the shipping supplies must meet rigorous environmental and health standards. As a result, the USPS expects to prevent more than 15,000 metric tons of carbon-dioxide-equivalent emissions annually.[10] Also, most post offices are equipped with an automated station where you can purchase postage for packages twenty-four hours a day, seven days a week. That means you can skip the long line or go to the post office whenever it is most convenient for you. In addition, you probably won't have

to travel nearly as far to go to the post office as you would to ship through another shipping company. And best of all, if you have envelopes and boxes at home, you can calculate and print postage from there (visit USPS.com).

22. MAKE CORPORATIONS RESPONSIBLE

Many businesses recognize the effect they have on the environment and are changing their operations to lessen the impact. Some businesses have assessed the carbon footprint of their organizations, even completing a life cycle analysis (LCA) for some of their products. Some companies are reducing their carbon footprint as much as possible before purchasing quality offsets, and only work with suppliers that meet certain emission standards. When purchasing products, first consider how the company producing the good or service is impacting the environment and what they are doing to make a difference. Many companies make their corporate sustainability reports (CSRs) available on their websites. A CSR is sometimes used to document a company's efforts to lessen its impact on the environment and reduce its carbon footprint.

Most of us don't have time to research all the companies out there, but fortunately the organization Climate Counts has produced a convenient scorecard that fits in your wallet. The scorecard ranks companies as either *striding, starting,* or *stuck* in their efforts to reduce their impact on the climate. The scorecard can be found at www.ClimateCounts.org. The next time you go shopping, take the scorecard with you so you can support companies that reflect your values.

*Because we don't think about
future generations, they
will never forget us.*[11]

Henrik Tikkanen

AT HOME

Did you know that at a fossil-fuel-burning power plant, producing the electricity needed to power a single home creates more carbon dioxide emissions than two average automobiles? Making your home more energy efficient not only reduces your carbon footprint, it can also save you money by reducing your utility bills from 10% to 50%. Begin by preparing your home to be energy efficient in order to maximize the use of the energy you're already paying for. After all, you don't want the air that was just heated or cooled (depending on the season) to leak right out the windows, doors, and roof. That's like throwing money out the window!

As every homeowner already knows, you can always improve your home. In fact, improving any home is typically an unending process. Your house may be over a hundred years old and need a great deal of maintenance and care, or you may be fortunate enough to have purchased an extremely energy-efficient home. Either way, once your home is as energy efficient as economically feasible, follow the simple suggestions in this section to conserve energy on a daily basis.

Beware of little expenses; a small leak will sink a great ship.[12]

Benjamin Franklin

Getting Started

23. PERFORM A HOME ENERGY AUDIT

Begin making your home more energy efficient by performing a home energy audit. An energy audit involves determining the energy efficiency of your home and considering improvements that will improve efficiency. The thought of making more improvements to your home may make you cringe, but many of the suggested improvements have a minimal cost or end up saving you money. (For example, if you need a new appliance for your home and are trying to decide between an energy-efficient model or a less-expensive, less-efficient model, in most cases, the energy-efficient model will end up costing less money due to operation costs over its lifetime.)

The energy audit will not take much time and will provide a foundation upon which to base your energy-improvement decisions. If you're game, you can probably perform the energy audit on your own. Otherwise, you may want to check with your local utility companies, as some of them provide energy audits either at no cost or for a minimal fee. Energy audits provide a way for you to determine which areas of your home are losing the most energy. From the audit, you will receive a list of recommendations for cost-effective energy improvements. Once you have identified the areas that need improvements, you can formulate a plan and assign priorities according to your budget and energy needs.

24. THE REFRIGERATOR

Of all the appliances and electronics in your home, the refrigerator uses the most energy (unless you have a spa or pool). A study of over 41,000 models of refrigerators and freezers manufactured between 1979 and 1992 found that the average refrigerator/freezer uses about 1,117 kWh per year.[13] However, Energy Star qualified refrigerators and freezers typically use less than half the energy as refrigerators and freezers manufactured before 1993.[14] Less electricity usage translates to a savings of $525 to $1,050 over the fifteen-year life of an energy-efficient refrigerator.

If you don't plan to replace your refrigerator in the near future, there are some things you can do now to reduce the energy your current refrigerator uses. Start by setting the temperature of your refrigerator at 35° to 38° F and the freezer at 5° F to conserve energy and still keep your food fresh. Also, make sure that the door of your refrigerator is sealed properly. To test the seal, place a dollar bill halfway in the refrigerator and close the door. If you can pull the dollar bill out easily, the seal may need to be replaced.

When I was young and would stand in front of the refrigerator staring blankly into it, my dad would tell me to close the door. At the time, I didn't understand why, but now I do. Minimizing the amount of time the refrigerator door is open saves energy. In addition, regularly defrosting your freezer (when the frost builds up beyond a quarter of an inch) will increase the freezer's efficiency. You can also conserve energy by allowing hot foods to cool at room temperature before putting them in the refrigerator, as long as this can be accomplished without causing any food-safety concerns.

Make sure your refrigerator is positioned away from heat sources, and leave a space between the back of the refrigerator and the wall to allow air to circulate around the condenser coils. Don't keep the fridge in the garage, as it will use more energy during both the summer and the winter. It is important to recycle old refrigerators and freezers, since they contain HFCs (greenhouse gases) that require special handling. Power companies know that old refrigerators and freezers are energy hogs, so many power companies will pick up an old refrigerator or freezer and even give you a bit of money for it or a credit on your power bill. Maybe it's time to reconsider how important the second freezer is to your household and if you can possibly do without it.

25. USE POWER STRIPS

Have you ever noticed that when you turn off an electronic device, sometimes a little red or green light remains on, meaning the electronic device is on standby?

Although you may think the device is off, it's still using energy while in standby mode. The most common culprits are televisions, DVD players, VCRs, surround-sound systems, satellite receivers, cable TV boxes, video games, computers, and microwave ovens. These are items that you probably don't use twenty-four hours a day, but by leaving them plugged in, you're still paying for energy you're not using. What's the solution? Instead of plugging in an electronic device each time you use it and unplugging it afterward, plug the devices that you use most frequently into a power strip. This would work well for your entertainment area. You can plug your television, surround-sound system, and satellite or cable TV receiver into a power strip, then turn them all on or off at the flip of a switch. You could have a separate power strip for your DVD player and VCR or game system since you probably don't use these as often as the television, or perhaps you're like me and you only like to watch DVDs on the television. Whatever the case may be, you can set up the power strips in a way that is most convenient for you.

Your computer is probably already plugged into a power strip with a surge protector. If not, it would be a good idea to do so to prevent the possibility of a power surge wiping out your hard drive. Some people think that they should leave their computer on all day long; however, this practice causes more wear on the computer, so unless you're working on your computer all day, remember to turn it off when you finish using it. Next time you shut your computer down, remember to turn off the power strip too. Power strips are not expensive and you will recoup the cost quickly by the energy you'll save on your next power bill.

26. USE COMPACT FLUORESCENT LAMPS (CFLs)

From your energy audit you've probably discovered the areas of your home where you use lighting most frequently. Replacing just 25% of the lightbulbs in these areas with compact fluorescent lamps (CFLs) will cut your energy use for lighting in half! Begin by replacing regular bulbs with CFLs in high-use areas, then gradually replace the bulbs in other areas of your home until you only use CFLs. Fluorescent lightbulbs use 75% less energy than incandescent bulbs and last up to 10 times longer, so even if you pay a little more for them up front, they will quickly pay for themselves and then some. If you use halogen lamps, you could replace them with compact fluorescent torchieres, which use 60% to 80% less energy. In addition, halogen lights tend to produce a lot of heat and can be fire hazards; CFLs are safer to use because they do not get nearly as hot. (This could also make a small difference in your air-conditioning use in the summer.) The expanded lifetime of CFLs is particularly useful for lights that are difficult to reach or replace.

Compact fluorescent lightbulbs do contain a very small amount of mercury. There is a bit of controversy over using CFLs because of the mercury, but until technology improves, the benefits far outweigh the risks as long as the bulbs are disposed of properly. To prevent mercury contamination, dispose of compact fluorescents at the appropriate recycling or disposal area. To identify local recycling centers for CFL disposal, go to www.epa.gov/bulbrecycling or www.earth911.org.

27. PROPERLY INSULATE YOUR ATTIC

Properly insulating your home is one of the best ways to reduce energy loss. Any money spent on insulation is usually recouped by the savings in heating or cooling the home. Insulation helps keep the house warm during the winter and cool during the summer. First, check the insulation in your attic. (If your home is older, your attic is probably not adequately insulated.) Compare the current amount and rating of the insulation with the recommended amount of insulation for your zone or area of the country. The Department of Energy has established six zones in the U.S. Most home improvement stores will be able to help you determine which insulation rating should be used in your area.

If you do not have adequate insulation in your attic, you can purchase cellulose insulation from your local home improvement store. Cellulose insulation is made from recycled wood fiber and recycled newspapers, then treated with fire retardants and insect repellant. If you want to install the insulation yourself, most home improvement stores have insulation blowers for rent. Blowing insulation into an attic takes two people and can be easily accomplished in about half a day. Working with cellulose insulation is easier and better than working with fiberglass, because it's much safer to touch and breathe.

A thick layer of insulation in the attic reduces the amount of heat that flows from the house to the attic, and during the summer, the attic insulation reduces the transfer of heat from the attic to the rooms below, keeping your home both warmer during the winter and cooler during the summer. You'll notice

a significant decrease in your energy bill when you go from inadequate to adequate insulation in your attic, making the purchase of the insulation money well spent.

28. WEATHERIZE YOUR HOME

Stop losing warm air during the winter and cool air during the summer by weatherizing your home. Weatherization entails sealing all openings in ceilings, walls, and floors where air can escape. You've probably already identified some areas of your home that have air leaks, but an easy way to check is to run your hand along window and door seals to check for air transfer. Checking for leaks is much easier on a particularly cold or windy day. Other places to check for leaks are electrical outlets, light switches (especially outlets and switches located on exterior walls), recessed lights, and dropped ceilings. Unfinished areas of a home are especially partial to air leaks and inadequate insulation. Also, walls adjoining the garage may be prone to air leaks. Before you start fixing leaks, you may want to write down where the leaks are or use some other kind of identification so you don't miss any.

Weatherization is quite simple. To fix leaks in electrical outlets and light switches, install a rubber gasket behind the switch or outlet to reduce air flow. Make sure you use the proper insulation around electrical areas to prevent a possible fire. For doors and windows, weatherstripping is an inexpensive and easy way to properly seal leaks. Caulk and seal gaps in exterior walls, and in ceilings and floors where holes exceed what is required for plumbing, air ducts, and electrical wiring. Homes still need to breathe, so be sure not to obstruct or seal vents that are necessary for proper ventilation.

29. INSTALL PROGRAMMABLE THERMOSTATS

There are many benefits of a programmable thermostat that make it worth the cost. The amount of money you will save on heating and cooling will more than pay for the new thermostat, not to mention reduce the amount of energy used and thus your carbon footprint. Unlike old thermostats, programmable thermostats do not contain mercury and are more accurate.

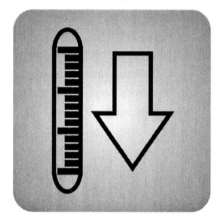

Your heater or air conditioner may be running when you aren't even home, so make sure that your programmable thermostat has multiple settings during the day and distinguishes weekdays from weekends. If you have a set work schedule, program your thermostat so you don't waste energy when you aren't home. At night, when you're usually sleeping, reduce the temperature setting on your thermostat and add a blanket or two to your bed. You can program your thermostat to heat the house in the morning when you're preparing for the day and then to shut off when you're not home. When you plan to go on vacation, you can program the thermostat to stay at a minimum temperature while you're away. Even though your thermostat may be programmed for a certain schedule, you can override the temperature when your plans change, then simply resume the normal schedule again as needed.

30. EVALUATE YOUR OUTDOOR LIGHTING

Outside lighting can be enjoyable, especially during the holidays, and it is sometimes an absolute necessity. Many people keep outside lights on all night for security reasons or throughout the holiday season. Although this may be considered wasteful by some people, there is a way to make everyone happy. Timers for outside lights can be easily installed on your light switch to control when outside lights turn on and off. If you adjust the timers with the seasons, you can ensure that your lights are not on when there is sunlight. If you use outdoor lighting for security reasons, timers can be very useful for turning your outdoor lights on even when you are away on vacation. Even better, you can use outdoor lights with photocell units so they will turn off automatically during the day.

Instead of leaving your outside lights on all night, consider using motion-detector lights, which only turn on when someone approaches the light. Motion-detector lights can also be useful in access areas, like the front door, so that the lights turn on whenever someone approaches your home. Some lights use photovoltaic (PV) modules, which are powered by solar energy, so they are off during the day and use only solar energy to stay lit during the night. These PV lights are relatively inexpensive and can be used to light walkways. Whichever outside lighting options you choose, try to be conscientious and conserve energy.

31. USE SUSTAINABLE BUILDING MATERIALS

If you decide to remodel your home, build an addition, or build a new home, consider using sustainable building materials and sustainable building practices. Using sustainable building materials promotes the conservation of nonrenewable resources, reduces waste, and conserves energy. Sustainable building materials may be taken from a renewable source, such as bamboo, or developed from recycled materials, such as 100% post-consumer recycled glass countertops and tiles. Salvaged materials from old buildings can also be used for new projects. When building, it's just as important to dispose of used building materials responsibly as it is to purchase sustainable building materials. For more information about sustainable building, visit the following websites: buildinggreen. com; greenhomebuilding.com; salvageweb.com; build.recycle.net; greenbuilding. com/sourcebook.

32. PURCHASE GREEN POWER

Green power is power that is sourced from a renewable resource such as wind, solar, biomass, or geothermal energy. Some power companies offer the option to purchase green power for a small premium. By purchasing green power, you are supporting the implementation of more renewable energy projects. Also, the more energy produced by renewable resources, the less we rely on fossil-fuel-burning sources of power—and the fewer greenhouse gas emissions we create.

When you purchase green power, it does not necessarily mean that the power from the renewable energy source will be directed straight to your home. Most of our homes are connected to a grid electrical system that transmits power throughout states and regions of the country. It does mean, however, that the additional charge you are paying goes directly to the purchase of renewable energy and supports new renewable energy development. By supporting clean, renewable energy in your region of the country, you are making a difference to help lessen our dependence on fossil fuels, improve the air quality, protect our health, and preserve the environment for future generations.

Call your local power company and inquire about purchasing power from renewable energy sources. If they do not offer the option to purchase green power, you can support programs through companies like Native Energy (Nativeenergy. com). Native Energy offers the opportunity to purchase offsets, allowing you to balance out your consumption of non-renewable energy by investing in renewable energy elsewhere. The money from the offsets you purchase is used to directly support the development of renewable energy in our country.

33. PLANT A GARDEN

Depending on where you live, you may be able to plant fruit trees and grow herbs and vegetables in your own backyard. Nothing from the grocery store tastes as good as fresh food from your own garden. If you are discouraged when it comes to buying organic fruits and vegetables from the grocery store due to the cost, try growing your own organic garden. Even if you live in an urban area or don't have a yard, herbs and tomato plants can be grown in small pots on a balcony or in a window flower box.

Gardening can benefit your household by providing fresh foods, and it can also serve as a relaxing hobby, nurturing both your body and soul. Watching the transformation and growth from seeds into fruits, vegetables, and herbs is also enjoyable. Extra food can be dehydrated or canned for off-season consumption and shared with your family, friends, and neighbors. Using the food from your own garden is an easy way to eat foods in season and avoid buying produce imported from other countries. It doesn't get more local than cultivating food in your own backyard, and you can't beat the price.

34. TURN DOWN YOUR WATER HEATER

Heating water in your home can constitute as much as 15% to 20% of your entire utility bill. However, for every 10°F you reduce your water heater thermostat, you can decrease your energy bill by 3% to 5%. Check your thermostat: a temperature above 130°F is unnecessary, and a setting of 115°F can prevent injuries but still provide warm showers. Also, installing non-aerating, low-flow faucets and showerheads will reduce the consumption of hot water in your home.

Much of the heat from hot water can be lost through exposed water pipes. Insulating your hot water pipes, as well as the entire water heater, can reduce the amount of heat that is lost while the water is being heated and distributed to different areas of the home. Review the safety precautions in your water heater manual before adjusting the thermostat and insulating the unit.

If you need to replace your water heater, consider installing a solar-powered water heater or a tankless water heater that only generates hot water when it is needed. Tankless water heating systems conserve energy by only heating water when it is needed instead of constantly maintaining the heat of a fifty-gallon tank of water. If you've decided to purchase a conventional water heater instead, be sure to buy the size appropriate for your household size. Also, look for a water heater that includes a heat trap and is well insulated.

Remember, if you're going on a vacation and won't be home for a while, make sure to turn down the water heater. Some water heaters even have a "vacation" setting on the thermostat. If you'll be away for three days or more, you can turn an electric water heater off at the circuit breaker. However, if you're leaving during the wintertime and your water heater is the only source of heat in your basement, turning the water heater off completely could cause the pipes to freeze. In this case, just turning the water heater down is a better option. Although we rarely think about the water heater, it consumes a lot of energy in our home, but we can take steps to conserve the amount of energy used to heat water in our homes.

35. RECONSIDER YOUR LANDSCAPING STRATEGY

Landscaping your yard is a beautiful and effective way to reduce energy use in your home and increase the property value. By positioning trees, shrubs, and vines to provide shade and block the wind, you can reduce the amount of energy needed to keep your home comfortable. The Department of Energy estimates that just three properly placed trees can save the average household $100 to $250 annually in heating and cooling energy costs.

The landscaping strategy you should use depends on the type of climate you live in. If you live in an area with hot summers and cold winters, plant deciduous trees to shelter your home from heat during the summer. When the trees lose their leaves, the sun can then warm your home during the cold months. Placed on the north and west sides of a home, evergreen trees can block winter winds; placed on the south and west sides, they can deflect summer winds.

In conjunction with a light-colored roof, trees planted around your home are a great way to absorb reflected sunlight from your home. When water evaporates from the trees surrounding your home, it actually cools the air near the trees. Also, using native plants and trees will reduce the amount of water required to maintain the plants and promote a healthy ecosystem in your yard. The benefits of landscaping are numerous. When designing the landscaping surrounding your home, consider the impacts from the climate and how to reduce exposure by planting smart to save energy.

36. REDUCE ENERGY USED FOR POOLS, SPAS, OR HOT TUBS

Pools, spas, and hot tubs require a pump to power the filtration system that helps keep the water clean. For a spa or hot tub, heating is also required, making the spa or hot tub the highest energy consumer in your home. (Pools come in second.) In fact, a typical spa uses about twice the amount of electricity as a common refrigerator.

Unless you're like my parents, who own a hot tub but never even fill it with water, you're probably wondering what you can do to reduce the amount of electricity used by your pool, spa, or hot tub. You can start by using a timer for the pool pump to control and decrease the amount of time the pump is in use. Check the instruction book for the filtration system to find out how long the pump needs to run each day. You can also determine the proper amount of time by reducing the amount of time your pool pump runs by one hour. If the pool water is still clean in three days, try reducing it by another hour and repeat this process until you have reached the minimal amount of time necessary for the pool pump to operate but still clean the water adequately. Then adjust the pool pump timer according to the season and environment. Less filtration time is needed during winter months or whenever the pool is not in use for extended periods. Also, keeping the filtration system clean reduces the energy needed to keep your pool clean.

Conserve the heat generated for a heated pool, spa, or hot tub by covering it when not in use. Be sure to use a tight-fitting, insulated cover. A cover will also reduce evaporation. Spas and hot tubs can also be insulated around the sides and bottom before—and sometimes after—installation. If you rarely use your spa or hot tub, lower the temperature to 60° to 80°F (depending on frequency of use and the outside temperature) when it is not in use. When you go on vacation, turn off the heater for the pool, spa, or hot tub. You can also supplement the heater with a solar heater, thereby taking advantage of free, clean, natural energy.

Wood-fired hot tubs are gaining popularity and only require heating when you use them. A friend of mine made his own hot tub by filling an old cattle trough with water and heating it with a wood fire. It's not necessary to be this rustic to enjoy a hot tub or pool without a guilty conscience, but try to use the minimal amount of energy to maintain your pool or hot tub.

37. INSULATE YOUR DUCTS

You probably don't think much about the hidden ducts in the walls, floors, and ceilings of your home, but the duct system plays an important role in your home. Ducts move hot air from the furnace and cold air from the central air conditioner throughout your home. Insulating and sealing any leaks in these ducts can save you hundreds of dollars annually on your utility bills. If ducts are leaking, heated and cooled air is forced out of unsealed joints. Since the ducts are typically installed in walls, under floors, and in ceilings, any leaked air doesn't contribute much to the heating and cooling of your home. Also, outside air can be drawn into leaks, causing the furnace or air conditioner to operate longer and use more energy, which costs more money and causes more emissions. It may be necessary to get a professional technician to check for leaks and insulate ducts located in areas that are difficult to access. However, if you have an unfinished area in your home or have drop ceilings, the ducts are more accessible and you may be able to repair and insulate yourself. If you're really motivated, you can also clean the inside of the ducts and remove obstructions, which will also increase air flow and efficiency. If not, there are companies that specialize in cleaning air ducts. Cleaning air ducts also improves the air quality in your home, helping decrease symptoms of allergies and asthma.

38. DO NOT USE PLASMA TELEVISIONS

Even if Super Bowl Sunday is coming up, resist the urge to compete with your neighbors, and just say no to plasma televisions. The *Wall Street Journal* recently stated, "A 42-inch plasma television set can consume more electricity than a full-size refrigerator—even when that TV is used only a few hours a day."[15] This means that your new plasma television could cost you about $200 per year just in electricity alone. Unless your home is completely powered by renewable energy, that's a lot of greenhouse emissions just to watch TV.

High-definition LCD televisions are comparable to plasma televisions as far as picture quality, but LCD televisions use much less energy. In fact, an LCD television typically uses about 30% less power than a plasma television of the same size. LCD televisions are priced competitively with plasma televisions and tend to have a higher native screen resolution. Also, on average, LCD televisions have a lifespan that is double that of plasma televisions.

Plasma televisions can have screen burn-in, which happens when a picture is on the screen for an extended period of time, whereas LCDs do not have this problem.

When shopping for a new television, take into account the amount of energy the television will need in order to operate. Even better, make sure that any television you purchase has an Energy Star sticker. And don't forget to use a power strip so you can keep your television off when not in use, instead of letting it suck power in standby mode. Also consider reducing the number of televisions in your home by donating a television (or two or three) to a local thrift store. You may be surprised by how much you won't miss your television. According to the *American Journal of Public Health,* an adult that watches three hours of television per day is much more likely to be overweight than an adult that watches less than an hour.[16] So just shutting off the television may be the best and easiest diet plan. Sounds great, doesn't it? Lose a few pounds *and* save energy!

39. USE A DEHUMIDIFIER

If you live in a very humid area, dehumidifiers can help prevent damage to your home and health. However, a dehumidifier can use almost as much energy as an air conditioner. If you use a dehumidifier in your home, check the level of your humidistat. The humidistat regulates humidity just as a thermostat regulates temperature. If the humidistat is set to its lowest setting, the dehumidifier will run continuously. Since there is no real benefit from the dehumidifier working overtime, it is just wasting energy. Adjust the humidistat to the highest level that will still provide adequate dehumidification. This will result in the unit only running intermittently, saving electricity.

That which we persist in doing becomes easier for us to do; not that the nature of the thing itself has changed, but that our power to do it has increased.[17]

Ralph Waldo Emerson

Chores and Relaxation

40. HANG YOUR CLOTHES TO DRY

In the United States, clothes dryers account for 6% to 10% of total residential electricity consumption. In fact, just one T-shirt can cause up to nine pounds of carbon dioxide emissions over its lifetime due to washing and drying.[18] Multiply that by the number of clothing items you have in your closet, and that adds up to a lot of greenhouse gas emissions for just one individual. Getting back to basics by hang-drying clothes can save a lot of energy and reduce your carbon footprint.

Growing up, I remember helping my sisters hang our family's laundry outside on the clothesline. I loved the smell of freshly dried clothes as well as being outside in the sun as we took the laundry down and folded it. For some reason, we started using a clothes dryer, but I don't have any good memories from cleaning the lint out of the dryer.

I now hang-dry my clothes for numerous reasons. First, using a clothes dryer wears clothing out sooner and can also shrink your favorite shirt or pair of pants. The high heat and tumbling action of the dryer breaks down fibers and deteriorates clothing. (The lint you have to clean out of the dryer is proof of this.) Second, I don't have to wait around for my laundry to finish drying so that I can fold it as soon as the dryer stops. Instead, once my laundry is washed, I hang it up. Then I'm free to do as I wish without worrying that my clothes will wrinkle from sitting in the dryer too long. Also, my clothes can go directly into my closet once they're dry, since I've already hung them up. If I forget about my clothes for a few days once they are hung, it doesn't matter. Third, in the winter, I hang-dry my clothes indoors. The furnace depletes the home's air of moisture, and the clothes add moisture back into the air as they dry. If you don't have a shower rod to hang the clothes on, they will still dry outdoors even if it is cold or cloudy (as long as it isn't raining, of course). If you still want to fluff up your clothes in the dryer, do so after they've air-dried. It will only take a few minutes and use a lot less energy.

41. USE COLD WATER TO WASH CLOTHES

When I lived in the rainforest in Costa Rica, we collected fresh rainwater for all our needs, including the laundry, which meant all of our loads were washed in cold water. I was baffled by the concept of no hot water, especially when it came to showering. Nonetheless, I soon adapted to taking cold showers, even though I secretly dreamed of the warm showers I was used to. I'm not suggesting that we all start taking cold showers, but we can easily wash all of our laundry in cold water.

Using cold water to wash clothes simplifies the task of sorting laundry. You don't have to worry so much about dividing your laundry into specific colors, because washing in cold water prevents most laundry from "bleeding" or emitting dye. In fact, I can separate my laundry into two large loads; whites and colors. This also eliminates the need to wash small loads of laundry. Many detergents are specifically made for washing clothes in cold water. In fact, cold water detergent can clean your clothes in cold water just as well as they would be cleaned in warm water. Since 90% of the energy used by a washing machine comes from heating the water, using cold water and only washing full loads of laundry conserves a great deal of energy.[19]

42. REDUCE YOUR NEED TO IRON CLOTHING

You may need crisply ironed clothing for work or other events, and air drying doesn't usually prevent wrinkles in fabrics such as cotton and linen. But if you hang your clothes in the bathroom while you shower, the steam will eliminate some or all of the wrinkles, making ironing unnecessary. If you find that some items of clothing still need ironing, iron large batches of clothing at a time, instead of using energy to heat the iron every time you need to iron a single article of clothing. If you only have a few items that need ironing, try putting them in the dryer for about five minutes (check the label first to make sure the fabric will not shrink or be damaged). Also, when you shop for new clothing, look for items that are "wrinkle-free" and that don't require dry cleaning. (Even though the label may say "Dry Clean Only," sometimes an article of clothing can be hand washed and air dried.) Furthermore, steaming dry-clean-only clothes in the bathroom will also help eliminate odors and reduce wrinkles.

43. USE YOUR DISHWASHER MORE EFFICIENTLY

If you have a dishwashing machine, you can still conserve energy and get clean dishes. Most of the energy used by the dishwasher is for heating the water. Most dishwashers are equipped with internal heating elements to heat the water, which means you can set your water heater at a lower temperature and it won't affect the temperature used by the dishwasher. Newer dishwashers are more energy efficient than earlier models, meaning they use less hot water and consequently less energy. Some of us find it necessary to rinse or wash the dishes before putting them in the dishwasher. If you're going to go to that length, you might as well just wash the dishes by hand and use the racks in the dishwasher for drying purposes only. If your dishwasher isn't washing dishes that haven't been washed already, it's probably time to get a repair person to look at it.

If your dishwasher is working properly, you should only need to scrape excess food off dishes instead of rinsing or washing them before putting them in the dishwasher. Otherwise, it takes about twice the amount of hot water to both rinse your dishes and wash them in the dishwasher. Of course, some dishes may need to soak in water if food has been burned or dried onto the dish. But much hot water can be conserved by skipping the rinsing before putting dishes in the dishwasher.

Most dishwashers have the option to use heat to dry the dishes. If you turn this option off and let your dishes air-dry by opening the dishwasher door a bit, you're conserving even more energy. The "rinse hold" option on your dishwasher is usually unnecessary and can waste three to seven gallons of hot water each time you use it.[20] Also, reduce the number of loads you wash by making sure the dishwasher is completely full before starting it. If you have a large household, you may have inadvertently washed a load of dishes twice if you were unaware that they were already washed. My mother uses a small magnet on her dishwasher that says "clean" or "dirty" to avoid washing the dishes twice. This works really well, especially now that my mother is getting older and has difficulty remembering if she started the dishwasher or not. Of course, if you don't rinse or wash the dishes before putting them in the dishwasher, it is much easier to distinguish whether the dishes have been through a washing cycle or not.

44. USE LESS WATER WHEN HAND-WASHING DISHES

Many of us don't have automatic dishwashers or prefer to wash dishes by hand. Washing the dishes by hand can be a relaxing and enjoyable task, especially if you like to clean when nervous or angry to blow off some steam. I don't have to be angry to clean the house, but being upset does motivate me.

It is possible to conserve hot water and still get the dishes sparkling clean. The following process offers a way to save energy while washing dishes by hand. Begin by closing up the drain in the sink and adding a couple of inches of hot water along with a bit of liquid dish soap. This amount of water is enough to wash glasses and silverware. After washing these items, rinse them over the same side of the sink as the soapy water. This will slowly add water to the sink to wash larger items. Or, if you use the adjacent sink to rinse dishes by dipping them in clean, cool rinse water, you can save about $100 a year.[21] Or you can stack plates in the adjacent sink so that as you rinse one plate, the water that runs off will rinse the plate below it. There are many methods for hand-washing dishes, but whichever method you choose, try to conserve hot water.

45. TAKE SHORTER SHOWERS

I have four sisters, and while growing up in the same household, we all loved taking long showers. Of course, no one could flush the toilet or run the hot water at the same time without hearing the person in the shower scream, "Turn off the water!" If you were the youngest and at the end of the line like me, you would end up taking a cold shower. My dad was in the U.S. Navy and thought the solution was taking showers the same way he did when he was on a ship. They had to conserve water on the ship, so they were only allowed to shower for one minute or less. They would turn on the water to get wet, shut it off while they lathered up, and then turn the water on just long enough to rinse off the soap. I wish my sisters had mastered the navy shower. If they had, I would have enjoyed more hot showers during my youth.

Perhaps you aren't as frugal as my father, but reducing the amount of time you spend in the shower can save a great deal of hot water. Start by turning the water off while you shave in the shower or lather up. Some showerheads allow you to shut off the water at the nozzle so you don't waste water but still keep the water at the same temperature. Taking brief showers instead of taking baths also conserves hot water, unless you like to bathe in only a couple inches of warm water.

46. DON'T FILL THE BATHTUB

Bathing can be a wonderful way to relax and pamper yourself. Indulging in the occasional bubble bath or using some Epsom salt to relax your muscles may be something you can't do without. Most children especially enjoy bath time, and bathing two kids at once can be quite efficient. If you have several children, you can clean a few with the same water, depending on how dirty they are.

The only way to conserve energy while bathing is to use less hot water. The tub doesn't need to be filled to the top, so try filling it a bit lower than usual. When I bathe, I like to fill up the tub just a couple inches and lather up while the bathtub fills. Then I add just a little hot water about every ten minutes to warm up the tub. That way I don't fill the tub beyond halfway, but I still get to enjoy a long, leisurely bath. When you bathe, you don't have to limit the amount of time you spend in the tub like you do in the shower, as long as you don't mind wrinkled toes and fingers. Also, after bathing during the winter, I leave the hot water in the tub to add moisture to the air and warmth to the home. (Be sure to consider the danger to small children if you do this.) You can also use the water to bathe the dog, clean something, or water the plants—depending on whether you used soap, etc.

47. USE CANDLES

Non-petroleum-based candles have many uses and can be used to conserve energy. They are a good alternative to plug-in air fresheners or toxic sprays. Plug-in air fresheners have become very popular; however, these fresheners constantly use electricity, and the refills sometimes cost more than the plug-in itself. Using candles is more economical. You probably don't unplug air fresheners every time you leave the house, and is it really necessary to scent the air in your home when you're sleeping or not even there?

Candles have many uses in addition to providing a nice aroma. Candles can also be used as lighting to create a romantic or relaxing atmosphere. It is also possible to make your own candles at home, which can become an enjoyable hobby. Homemade candles also make great gifts. Storing candles in the freezer after you burn them will make the candles last even longer. Next time you need a little lighting or want to freshen the scent of your home, light a candle before plugging in an air freshener or flipping on a light (this may be a practice for after the kids are grown).

48. COOK IN BULK

Preparing large batches of food at one time is an excellent way to make the most out of the energy needed to prepare your meals. Instead of preparing many small meals every day, you can make one large meal and freeze the extra portions for another day. By preparing large meals at once, you can utilize food purchased in bulk quantities. This saves money, time, and energy. It can also be fun to invite family, friends, or neighbors to share the cost of bulk food, and then everyone can cook together and make enough food to freeze the portions they need. Some businesses facilitate the preparation of meals that can be frozen into particular quantities. This allows you to prepare the food according to their recipes in a timely manner. The store is usually set up in stations, similar to a buffet, except the food is not consumed onsite and you only pay for what you want. At franchises such as My Girlfriend's Kitchen, you can prepare your own meals. (To find a location near you, check the website: www.mygirlfriendskitchen.com.) In many families, both parents work full time. Preparing several meals in advance is a great way to quickly serve a wonderful meal later. After a long day at work, a quick and easy meal will be that much more enjoyable.

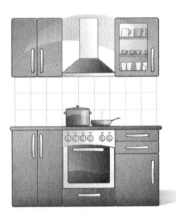

*If future generations are to
remember us with gratitude rather
than contempt, we must leave
them something more than the
miracles of technology. We must
leave them a glimpse of the world
as it was in the beginning, not just
after we got through with it.*[22]

Lyndon B. Johnson

Cooling Your Home

49. USE AIR FANS

Fans are an efficient and low-cost alternative to using an air conditioner for cooling your home. When air is circulated, a room feels cooler by several degrees. Whole-house fans, typically installed in the ceiling, are used to pull cool air through the house and push hot air out through the roof. Whole house fans are less expensive to install and to operate than air-conditioning units and only need to run for an hour or less in the evening to cool the entire house. Ceiling fans work in a similar fashion to pull cool air up and distribute it throughout the room. Ceiling fans can also be useful for keeping your home warm in the winter. Simply reverse the direction of the fan blades so warm air is pushed down into the room instead of escaping through the roof. If you live in a dry climate, misting fans are a great way to cool down a room while also increasing the moisture in the air.

In the evening after the sun has set, take advantage of cross-ventilation. On one side of your home, place fans positioned to blow hot air out of the windows. On the opposite end of the house, open the windows. The fans will blow out the hot air that has accumulated throughout the day while also creating a draft to pull cool air into the house from outside. Your home will stay cool throughout the night and even into the next morning. Cross-ventilation works especially well in some desert climates where it is hot during the day and cool at night. Unless you live in a very humid area or where the temperature doesn't vary much between daytime and nighttime, fans can cool your home very effectively for little cost.

50. MAXIMIZE THE EFFICIENCY OF YOUR AIR CONDITIONER

If you use either a room air conditioner or central air-conditioning, most of the energy you consume during the summer is from using the AC unit. In fact, many power companies strain to meet the summer demand for electricity driven by the increased use of air-conditioning units in homes. If you already have an air conditioner in your home, you're not expected to shut it down and stop using it altogether. However, there are ways to reduce the amount of electricity used by your AC unit while still being comfortable during hot summer days.

Placement of the air-conditioning unit and thermostat can make a big difference in energy consumption. Your air-conditioning unit is probably located outside. If you plant trees or shrubs around to shade the unit (without blocking air flow), you can reduce electricity use by up to 10%. Notice the area around the thermostat as well. If there are lights or a television or any other appliance that gives off heat when operating, the thermostat will sense the heat and will run longer than necessary. While you're checking out the thermostat make sure it is set to the warmest temperature that is still comfortable. Most people are comfortable with a setting of 78°F or even higher. For each degree the thermostat is set above 78°F, you'll save 6% to 8% in energy costs. If you set the AC to simply recirculate air, you'll conserve even more energy.

If you use a smaller air conditioner for cooling one area instead of the entire home, consider using a fan in conjunction with the AC unit to increase air flow and cool the area more effectively without significantly increasing your power use. Using fans in rooms instead of the system's central fan even works well for larger, whole-house units. That way you can also focus on only cooling the rooms you are using. If the AC circulates air through the ducts in your home, you can close the vents and the doors to the rooms you aren't using to reduce the amount of time the AC runs. Also, turn off the AC unit if you aren't using it, especially when you aren't home. Proper maintenance will improve the efficiency of your air conditioner and reduce energy costs. Clean or replace the air filters monthly and check outdoor units for any debris that may be obstructing the coils.

Did you know that a bigger air conditioner may not actually be better? In fact, if the air-conditioning unit is not properly sized for the area it is cooling, it will actually perform less efficiently and won't cool the room as effectively. AC units work most effectively when they run for an extended period to maintain a more constant room temperature. If the unit is oversized, it will use more power as it continually turns on and off, and it will not maintain a constant room temperature. Consult with a professional to determine the proper AC unit size for your home, or check the following website: http://www.energystar.gov/index.cfm?c=roomac.pr_properly_sized

51. IMPROVE YOUR WINDOWS

If you live in a warm climate year round or just have hot summers, there are things you can do to reduce the amount of heat that enters your home through your windows—double-paned or not. Using white or very light-colored window shades, drapes, or blinds can reflect the sun's heat away from your home. During the day, close the light-colored window coverings on the south- and west-facing windows to reflect heat away from your home and to reduce the load on the cooling system. Installing awnings on the south- and west-facing windows will also reduce the amount of heat coming in to your home. In addition, reflective films can also be applied to south-facing windows.

When you are ready to replace single-paned windows in your home, consider installing windows specifically made for warm climates, which are designed to reflect some of the sunlight. Double-paned windows provide extra insulation, which keeps hot air out during the summer and keeps warm air in during the winter. If you are unable to replace or upgrade all the windows in your home at once, start with the largest windows first, since larger single-paned windows allow more air to escape than do smaller windows. If you've ever stood or walked by a window in your home and felt a breeze or pocket of cold air, it may be time to replace the window or at least make sure it is sealed properly.

52. USE A SWAMP COOLER INSTEAD OF AN AIR CONDITIONER

Swamp coolers, also called evaporative coolers, are an efficient way to cool your home, since they use much less energy than air conditioners. However, swamp coolers only work in climates with relatively low humidity levels. Swamp coolers operate by pulling air through damp pads that are continually wetted by recirculating water. The heat in the air evaporates water from the pads, and the resulting cool, moist air is blown into the home through a vent. Secondary water or non-potable water (such as that used to water the lawn) can also be used to operate the swamp cooler instead of wasting treated water. A swamp cooler, which can be mounted on the roof or installed through a window, is much less expensive to purchase and operate than an air-conditioner. When a swamp cooler is running, opening a window at the opposite end of the house will create a flow of air that can cool the entire house. Furthermore, it's unnecessary to operate a swamp cooler when no one is home, because the cooler will start cooling the home as soon as it is switched on.

53. APPLY FENG SHUI IN YOUR HOME

Feng shui is the practice of arranging furniture and other items in such a way that creates harmony in your home. Try to apply this principle in terms of which areas of your home get the most use.

One easy way to conserve energy is to take advantage of the cooler areas of your home during hot days. A basement is usually much cooler than the main floor of a home, because hot air rises naturally and because a basement is typically more shaded from sunlight. Even if you don't have a basement, there may be areas of your home that are cooler because they are north facing or because of outside shade. If you live in a climate that is always warm or if you experience extremely hot summers, it may be worth rearranging your home so that the areas you use most are located in cooler areas of the home. For example, if you spend most of your time watching television or reading books, you may want to consider situating your library or television set in a naturally cooler area of your home. You can also close off areas of your home that you don't use as often by closing vents and doors, so that you aren't cooling areas unnecessarily. Use Feng shui in your home by situating your most-used furniture and other items in the most comfortable areas per the climate you live in. With proper placement, you'll save energy and enjoy more harmony in your home.

54. PROPERLY VENTILATE YOUR KITCHEN

When it's warm outside, cooking inside your home can create unwanted heat. However, proper kitchen ventilation can remove heat, odors, and humidity from your home. Range hoods or microwave ventilation can filter cooking grease and oil from the air, but they do not effectively remove heat and humidity from the kitchen. Using a vent that actually sends hot air directly to the outside of your home is more effective for removing cooking heat.

Using the oven and range less frequently during the summer, or cooking during cooler times of the day, can also reduce the amount of heat produced in the kitchen. When the weather is nice, take advantage of the barbeque grill and cook more foods outside. In addition, you can prepare meals that don't require cooking. Besides, eating something hot on a particularly warm day is probably not as enticing as it would be on a cold winter day. Creating less heat in the kitchen and properly venting heat are easy ways to reduce your summer energy use.

You must be the change you
wish to see in the world.

Mahatma Gandhi

Heating Your Home

55. DRESS WARMLY

During my childhood, if I complained in winter that our house was cold, my mom would retort, "Then put some clothes on." At the time, that wasn't the response I wanted, so I kept complaining even though she didn't turn the thermostat up. Eventually, I started dressing warmer inside and outside of the house and stopped complaining about it. In fact, I may have gone to the other extreme, because I keep my house a bit chilly nowadays, and my friends usually wear sweaters or keep their jackets on when they visit my home. They've also come to realize that complaining doesn't motivate me to turn up the heat. Fortunately, even though my home is a bit chilly, my friends haven't stopped visiting.

It is not necessary to make your home uncomfortably cold, but the next time you feel a little chilly, put on a sweater, socks, and slippers before turning up the heat. Keep a blanket near the couch or recliner. Make yourself something warm to drink or eat, or even better, cuddle up next to someone. My dog Max makes a great little lap heater, and it's hard to get him to move once he's comfortable. Even though the concept is very logical for most people, some of us still need to be reminded to dress appropriately for the climate we live in instead of adapting the temperature indoors to suit our style.

56. MAINTAIN YOUR FURNACE

Regular maintenance will help ensure that your furnace operates properly and efficiently. Simply checking and changing the air filter on a regular basis will improve the performance of the furnace and make it more energy efficient. Some furnace thermostats even remind you to change the filter. Most filters are inexpensive, and changing them is usually quick and easy.

Have a technician check the duct system in your home for leaks. Leaks can be sealed with special duct tape available at your local home improvement store. A service technician can also check the furnace fan to make sure it is operating correctly. If the fan thermostat is set incorrectly, the fan may stop running while the furnace is still operating. Consequently, the furnace is producing heat but isn't circulating the heated air through your home. Conversely, if the fan is running after the furnace shuts off, cold air will blow out the air ducts, countering the whole process of heating your home. A regularly maintained furnace operates much more efficiently than a poorly maintained furnace. Even if your furnace is old, make sure it is operating at maximum efficiency by performing regular maintenance.

57. CHECK FOR PROPER CALIBRATION

If you use natural gas to power your furnace, boiler, or water heater, make sure the appliance has a green sticker. If it doesn't, ask your natural gas supplier to provide an inspection. The green sticker means that the appliances has been checked and properly adjusted by a licensed contractor to ensure safe and efficient operation. If these appliances are not properly adjusted, carbon monoxide could be leaking into the home, leaving the occupants at risk. Carbon monoxide (not to be confused with carbon dioxide, the greenhouse gas) is a poisonous, odorless gas that is impossible for humans to detect with our senses alone. When it comes to protecting your family and home, a carbon monoxide alarm is just as important as a smoke detector. In addition to helping protect you from a carbon monoxide leak, an inspection can also ensure that you are not paying for more natural gas than your furnace is capable of using.

58. CONSIDER USING HEAT PUMPS

Heat pumps are the most efficient heating and cooling technology currently available. They can generate three times more heat than a regular heating system, using the same amount of energy. Geothermal heat pumps use only the earth's natural heat, but more versatile heat pumps can use either water, air, or ground sources for heating and cooling. Heat pumps can work both ways, either collecting and pumping heat into your home to warm it, or, conversely, collecting heat from your home and effectively pumping it back outside to cool your home. Make sure the heat pump is the proper size for your home and professionally installed by a licensed contractor—with proper insulation and air sealing to maximize efficiency. Heat pumps also require regular maintenance, including cleaning and filter replacement. Even though a heat pump has a higher up-front cost, the savings (a reduction on your electricity bill of 30% to 40%) will pay for the heat pump over time. The heat pump that will work best for your home will depend on where you live and which resources are available. If you are building a new home or considering new options for heating and cooling your home, include heat pumps on the list of options to explore.

59. AVOID GAS FIREPLACES

Gas fireplaces are a very expensive and energy-intensive way to heat your home. Most of the time, gas fireplaces are designed to create ambiance, not to heat a home, since most of the heat created escapes through the chimney. Gas fireplaces either have a standing pilot light (which means they are on all the time) or an electronic ignition switch. A continually burning pilot light wastes natural gas while the fireplace is not in use. If you don't use your gas fireplace every day, turn off the pilot light to conserve natural gas and reduce your utility bill. Especially during the summertime, when you probably never use your gas fireplace, shut the pilot light off completely. Check the instructions for your gas fireplace before shutting off or igniting your pilot light. Since a gas leak could have devastating consequences, ensure that the gas is turned off at the source before you light the pilot light or turn it off. Lighting and shutting off the pilot light after each use of the gas fireplace will

also make you more conscious of how often you use the gas fireplace and may even convert you to the occasional use of a wood-burning stove instead.

60. CLOSE DOORS AND VENTS

Unless there is only one room in your home, you're probably not using every area of your home all the time. Maybe you use certain rooms for only part of the day or a few days of the week, or maybe you have spare rooms that are only used when you have guests. If you have an unfinished basement that you don't use, close all the vents and perhaps even install a door at the bottom of the stairs to close the area off completely. Closing the doors and vents in the rooms you aren't using means heated air will only flow to the areas of the home that you use the most. When you do not have to heat your entire home, it will take less energy to keep it cozy. Your home will heat up much more quickly too, and the furnace won't need to run nearly as long to maintain the temperature. Conversely, you can close off the room of the home that you use most frequently and only heat that one room instead of heating the entire house.

61. TURN DOWN THE HEATER AT NIGHT

When you're cuddled up under some warm blankets at night, you are probably warm enough without the furnace running. Depending on how long you sleep, that's about eight hours that you don't need the heater. If you go to work another eight hours, that's two-thirds of each day that you don't have to heat your home. If

have a regular schedule, you can save money and energy by programming your thermostat to maintain a low setting during these periods of the day and night. Even if you don't have a programmable thermostat, make a habit of turning down the heat at night. You probably shouldn't shut your heater off completely, especially if it can get cold enough at night to freeze the pipes in your home. However, turning the thermostat down to 50° to 60°F should still allow you to be comfortable enough to get a good night's sleep, and high enough that you'll still conserve energy even though your heater may need to warm back up significantly during the day. Most people sleep better when the air is a bit cooler. If you have a small space heater in your bedroom, you could leave the thermostat at the same low setting while you prepare for work and use the space heater to heat your room briefly in the morning. That way you don't have to heat the entire house in the morning, and you can leave your thermostat down while you're out for the day.

62. TAKE ADVANTAGE OF THE SUN

During the winter, we typically spend more time indoors and use more electricity to light our home as we lose hours of daylight. Some people even develop a condition called seasonal affective disorder (SAD) as a result of being exposed to less sunlight in the winter. Letting the sunlight into your home during the day will reduce the need for electric lighting, and it will be reflected on your lower power bill. If you cover your windows with  plastic to reduce leaks, use clear plastic so that the sun can still shine through. The sunlight on the south, east, and west sides of your home will also help heat your home as well. Even though there is no heat benefit from opening the shades on the north side of your home, letting a little sunlight through will diminish the amount of time you need to turn on the lights. Besides, your body needs sunlight to get vitamin D. Letting a little sunlight in will brighten your spirits even on the coldest day.

63. SWITCH TO AN OUTDOOR FIRE PIT (VS. AN OUTDOOR HEATER)

Outdoor heaters, also called patio heaters, are commonly found on the patios of restaurants and even in backyards. Instead of staying indoors and dressing appropriately for the weather, some people actually try to heat the outdoors. Many retailers have already stopped selling patio heaters, and the U.K. wants to ban them completely. So, you may be wondering, why all the controversy? Patio heaters cause unnecessary emissions, with a single heater releasing, on average, almost four tons of greenhouse gases per year.[23] If you really enjoy staying outdoors in cold weather but want to have a source of heat, try building a fire instead of firing up the patio heater. I'm obviously not advocating starting a fire just anywhere using anything, but an occasional well-contained wood-burning fire pit can provide warmth without the additional greenhouse gas emissions. Because it also takes a bit more effort to start a fire than it does to ignite a patio heater, you probably won't be burning wood very often. Besides, patio heaters don't work very well unless you are directly below them. Even then, the planet is much better off if we all just wear warm coats outside.

64. OPEN THE OVEN DOOR AFTER BAKING

Wintertime is a time for family gatherings, holidays, and most importantly, lots of food. Whether you're baking food for a special occasion or no occasion at all, when you finish, remember to leave the oven open to send the excess heat and wonderful aroma into your home. Of course, if you have small children wandering around your home, it's probably not a good idea to leave the oven door wide open, but a small crack to vent will still do the trick. If you're preparing a lot of food, try to bake foods requiring similar temperatures at the same time to reduce energy consumption. If you have an electric range, even after you shut it off you can still keep food warm on top (instead of putting it on a simmer setting), or you can finish cooking an item with residual heat (especially useful when cooking oatmeal or grits) rather than wasting the heat after cooking. Also, use lids when cooking on the range to reduce the amount of energy and time needed for cooking.

65. USE THE FIREPLACE DAMPER

A fireplace typically has a damper, which closes off the airflow in the chimney. If you aren't using your fireplace, the heated or cooled air from your home is escaping up the chimney. Likewise, cold or hot air from outside is coming into your home through the chimney. Closing the damper when the fireplace is not in use will help prevent this. However, with any gas fireplace, the damper MUST remain open at all times to allow for safe venting of carbon monoxide gas, which can be deadly. Even if the pilot light on your gas fireplace is off, forgetting to open the damper can lead to carbon monoxide poisoning or even death. So to reiterate, if you have a gas fireplace, NEVER close the damper. However, you can install a tight-fitting cover (such as glass doors) on the gas fireplace, to reduce the amount of air flow between your home and the outdoors.

If you have a wood-burning fireplace, keep the damper closed when the fireplace is not in use. Make sure the damper is open when you have a fire going, and don't close the damper until the fire is completely out and the ashes are cold. Even a smoldering fire releases dangerous carbon monoxide, so err on the side of caution.

If you never use your wood-burning fireplace, you may want to consider sealing the area around the damper a bit better. This will reduce the amount of soot traveling into your home on windy days and will prevent air flow. If you do decide to seal the damper in your wood-burning fireplace, just make sure the seal isn't permanent and that it will be easy for the next homeowner to remove. And don't forget to tell the next homeowner about it!

66. SEAL YOUR DOORS

If the doors on the exterior walls of your home are not properly sealed, air will flow through your home, making it more difficult to heat and cool the house. On a particularly windy or cold day, you can test exterior doors for air leaks by moving your hand slowly around the seams. Also examine the weatherstripping around doorways to check for wear and to determine if it needs to be replaced. Proper sealing of doors can eliminate leaks and increase your heating efficiency. In addition, check the casing around unfinished doors for gaps. Sometimes inexpensive compression weatherstripping is all that is needed, while other times caulking or foam insulation may be required. Sometimes steel doors also have a magnetic weatherstripping along the top of the door and down the doorknob side.

Even if a door is bordered by trim, houses can settle a little over time, which often creates leaks. Check that the trim is still sealed, and if not, seal it with caulking. Don't forget the gap at the bottom of the door. If the door threshold is loose, it may need to be remounted or replaced. Door draft excluders can also be used under doors in the interior of your home to seal off rooms not being used or heated. You will need to take the exterior doors off their hinges so the weatherstripping or door threshold can be replaced, so make sure you check for air leaks and seal doors before winter arrives.

67. SEAL YOUR WINDOWS

An important part of heating a home efficiently is preventing heat loss. A great deal of heat can be lost through the windows. Have you ever walked by a window and felt a draft? If you have single-pane windows, upgrading to double-pane windows can be very expensive. If you rent, replacing the windows is probably not even an option. When I lived in a house that was over one hundred years old, I loved the original windows, so I would cover the windows (underneath the blinds) with heavy plastic during the winter and reuse the same plastic every year. Instead of buying the thin plastic marketed for covering windows, you can purchase painters' plastic in bulk. This thicker plastic is more durable, so you can reuse it every year. It is also less expensive.

My current home was built in the '60s, and I'm definitely not attached to the windows, but I also can't afford to upgrade them to more efficient double-pane windows. Instead, I purchased fabric and made curtains to cover the windows.

Heavy fabric can work like plastic to keep heat from escaping. Curtains can be used over blinds or bamboo shades to trap even more heat. Also, make sure that your windows are locked and sealed properly.

When dirt collects in a window track, the window may not close completely, meaning it probably isn't locked either. Most windows are made with compressible weatherstripping that is only engaged and sealed when the window is locked. A little cleaning can solve this problem, and it will make your home safer and more energy efficient.

68. GET OUT OF THE HOUSE

We tend to stay indoors more during the cold winter months. The amount of daylight is shorter, so we also tend to use more energy to light and heat our homes. A cold day can be a good excuse to vegetate in front of the television or computer. While this may be a nice escape once in a while, a daily habit of inactivity can be harmful to our health and well-being. Shorter and colder days don't mean we can't enjoy life outdoors. So get out of the house, and take your friends and family with you. On a regular basis, try to spend the entire day or most of the day outside. If you don't have snowshoes, you could rent a pair and go on a hike with a friend. If you live in the city, you could take an extended walk and bring your camera along. You may be surprised by the beauty of your own backyard. It might be fun to go ice skating on a nearby lake with friends and family members; just make sure the ice is thick enough. Some cities have outdoor ice-skating rinks. Or you could go tubing or sledding at a neighborhood park.

Above all, use your imagination. What did you enjoy most about winter when you were a child? Sharing those experiences with your children, grandchildren, cousins, or nieces and nephews can create a rewarding memory for all of you. Make the most of today—don't waste it! Not only will you have a wonderful day, you'll save energy because no one will be in your house, so you can turn down the thermostats and leave the lights, televisions, and computers off.

The bicycle is the most efficient machine ever created: Converting calories into gas, a bicycle gets the equivalent of three thousand miles per gallon.[24]

Bill Strickland

TRANSPORTATION

If you are like most Americans, transportation is the largest portion of your carbon footprint. Unless you never fly on airplanes and only ride a bicycle for transportation, there is probably some room for improvement in this part of your life. Since gas prices continue to rise, this section offers some tips for getting the most miles out of each gallon of gas you buy. And if you are getting better mileage, you are also generating less pollution per mile.

Driving your personal vehicle every day of the year can cause as much greenhouse gas emissions as taking two or three airplane flights. Since flying can be less expensive than driving, more people are traveling by air, which has a much greater impact on the climate than traveling on land. Transportation is a very important part of our daily lives and our lifestyles, but there are ways to make the means by which we travel less harmful to the environment.

Your grandchildren will likely find it incredible—or even sinful—that you burned up a gallon of gasoline to fetch a pack of cigarettes![25]

Paul MacCready, Jr.

Automobiles

69. DON'T LET YOUR CAR IDLE

Do you start your car to "warm it up" in the morning? Do you leave the car idling outside while you are inside preparing to leave? This is a bad habit that some of us have adopted on cold mornings. Not only does it waste gas and increase pollution, it may also lead to a stolen car! You make think your neighborhood is safe, but habitually leaving your car running makes your car an easy target. If you're running the car for the heat, wear a coat, gloves, and hat instead.

Unless the outside temperature is below freezing, it is unnecessary to warm up your car's engine before you drive it. Instead, drive your car slowly and gently for the first five minutes (which you probably do anyway if you live in a neighborhood) to warm up the car. If you are really concerned, let your car idle for about thirty seconds, but remember, an idling engine releases about twice as many exhaust fumes as a vehicle in motion. If you live where the temperature routinely drops below freezing, a block heater can warm your engine when it is not running.

It is a myth that turning your car off and on uses more gas than letting the car idle. In fact, an idling car uses much more fuel than a car in motion. This fact enticed a major shipping company to reduce the number of left turns on their delivery routes to minimize idling and save fuel. It's amazing how such a small thing like letting your car idle can add up.

So take it to the next level: if your car will be idle for more than ten seconds, turn off the engine. Turn it off the next time you're waiting for the bridge or a train, while waiting in the drive-thru, or stuck at a long stop light. Stuck in a traffic jam? Turn off the engine until traffic starts moving, or even better, avoid rush hour by working a bit later, starting a bit earlier, or running errands when the traffic is minimal.

70. MAINTAIN YOUR AUTOMOBILE TO SAVE FUEL

Simple maintenance measures can actually improve the performance of a vehicle and conserve gas by increasing the number of miles the vehicle can travel on a gallon of gas. Maintenance includes getting a regular tune-up for the engine and consistently checking the oil, air filter, and tires.

Check the air filter regularly to ensure that it is clean, because clogged air filters can cause the vehicle to burn more gas than necessary. Try using a reusable air filter, which will save you the money, energy, and time it would take to run to the store to buy a new filter every time it was dirty.

Each time you fill up your gas tank, check the

air pressure in the tires and the level of motor oil in the engine. If the pressure is low in the tires, your car will not operate as efficiently and will burn more gas. It's worth your while to spend a couple of quarters to keep the tires properly inflated. Keeping the tires properly aligned and rotated also improves gas mileage and extends the life of the tires. While you're at the gas pump filling up your tank, check the oil dipstick. If the oil level in your engine is low, the vehicle will not operate as efficiently and will use more gasoline than necessary. Make it a habit to check your vehicle's oil level and tire pressure every time you stop for gas.

71. USE SYNTHETIC OIL IN YOUR VEHICLE

Petroleum prices are skyrocketing, so make the most out of the gas and oil you buy by using only synthetic oil in your vehicle. According to Amsoil, a vehicle's gas mileage can improve from 4.5% to 15% if it runs on synthetic oil rather than petroleum-based oil. Even though synthetic motor oil may cost more initially, you'll recoup the difference and then some because synthetic motor oil doesn't break down like petroleum oil. Therefore, synthetic oil only needs to be changed once a year, compared to peteroleum oil, which requires changing every three months. Also, used synthetic motor oil can be recycled at most places that offer oil-changing services. Synthetic oil improves the performance of the engine and has many other advantages over conventional motor oil. For instance, synthetic oil reduces wear on the engine, keeps the engine cleaner, and protects the engine even when the vehicle is operating under extreme conditions and high temperatures. With all the benefits of synthetic oil, it is well worth the extra initial cost.

72. CARPOOL

Carpooling takes cars off the road, which means less air pollution and less traffic. Many states have a special carpool lane on freeways to accommodate and encourage carpooling. If you don't want to make the effort to pick up some friends or coworkers on the way to work in the morning, watching people in the carpool lane fly by you while you're stuck in traffic may motivate you to make a change. To encourage carpooling among employees, some businesses reserve good parking spaces for carpooling vehicles. If your employer doesn't do this, consider putting a note in the comment box or making the suggestion to your boss. If you are the boss, be an example by not only carpooling yourself but also implementing incentives for your employees to carpool.

Carpooling is a great way to save money, gain a bit more time for yourself, and spend less time driving. You can either alternate driving among the people in your carpool, or agree upon compensation for the driver if driving is not shared equally. Being a passenger is a great time to catch up on a little sleep, read the paper, or get to know other people in your community. Creating a carpool group from work can accommodate your work hours and make coordination easier since you all have the same destination and can communicate with each other at work. It may also inspire others to form their own carpool. To form a carpool, check with the state transit authority for a carpooling hotline, or consider free carpooling-connection services available online at www.erideshare.com or www.carpoolconnect.com.

73. OBEY THE SPEED LIMIT

If you have a lead foot, this will probably be your least favorite way to reduce your carbon footprint. While using highways and freeways can increase fuel efficiency because the car is kept at a constant speed, if you're accelerating beyond the speed limit, you are actually canceling out the fuel efficiency benefit and consuming more fuel than necessary. According to FuelEconomy.gov, every increase in speed of 5 mph above 60 miles per hour amounts to paying an additional $0.20 per gallon of gasoline or a decrease of fuel efficiency by about 7%. Take advantage of the cruise control and overdrive option on your vehicle to maintain a constant speed, maximize fuel efficiency, and simplify your driving experience on the highway or freeway. The car zooming past you probably will not reach the same destination much faster than you will. Speeding also increases your chances of getting into an accident. Give yourself some extra time so you will not feel rushed driving; that way you can avoid tickets, arrive safely, and maximize your fuel efficiency.

74. EXAMINE HOW YOU DRIVE

Where and how you drive can make a significant difference in the amount of gas your vehicle consumes. To maximize fuel efficiency, avoid aggressive driving moves, including sudden starts, sudden stops, quick acceleration, and revving of the engine. Obviously, drag racing rapidly sucks up gasoline. Accelerating slowly and planning ahead so you can reduce your speed gradually will help your car get better gas mileage. Vent air into your car instead of rolling down the windows when traveling at high speeds; this reduces air drag and thus decreases fuel consumption. Keeping the windows up also reduces your exposure to exhaust. Avoid dirt or gravelled roads, since driving on rough roads uses about one-third more fuel than traveling the same distance on a paved road.

75. EXECUTE WELL-PLANNED ERRANDS

Do you spend an entire day running errands around town? Planning your errands in advance can reduce the amount of time you spend in your car each week—and the distance you drive. By prioritizing and then coordinating your errands in a consecutive manner, you can plan a route that will eliminate backtracking and excess travel. Also, take advantage of your lunch hour by running errands on foot near your workplace (don't forget your canvas bags). If you have multiple errands, choose an area near your home with several stores in one place so you can quickly complete multiple tasks. Create a grocery list on your fridge and add to it daily so you can make just one trip to the grocery store per week and so you won't forget items, provided you remember to bring the list with you. If you are running multiple errands that include grocery shopping, save the grocery shopping for last at the store nearest your home; otherwise, the food could spoil while you're running other errands. Invite friends and family to join you on your errands and coordinate your day together—that way you can carpool and have a little more fun while you're out and about. In addition, you could share your plan and offer to pick up or drop off items for other members of your household during your day. A little planning ahead of time can make your day run a bit smoother and help you finish your errands in a more timely manner. After all, do you really want to spend your day off running around town?

76. DON'T CARRY EXCESS WEIGHT IN YOUR CAR

You may have heard the phrase "no junk in the trunk" in a different context, but taking the phrase literally can save gasoline and improve the efficiency of your vehicle. Are you driving around with your trunk full of stuff? All that extra weight makes your car less fuel efficient. Spend a little time removing all unnecessary items from the trunk and backseat of your vehicle. Unless you use an item daily or it is needed for safety reasons, you don't need to keep it in your car.

Using crates, bags, or boxes in your garage is a great way to store items that you need to bring with you only occasionally. For example, I store all of my ski gear (except for the skis, obviously) in an old milk crate. When I plan to go skiing, I put the crate and skis in the trunk of my car, and when I return home, I store the crate in my garage. Same goes for my biking, climbing, golfing, and camping gear. Unless I plan to golf every day, I store my golf clubs in the garage or house instead of leaving them in the trunk of my car all summer long. This is also a great way to keep your gear organized so that the next time you're up for an adventure you can just grab the crate and go, instead of rummaging through all your stuff and hoping you don't forget anything.

77. BUY RECYCLED OR REFURBISHED PARTS

At the end of a vehicle's life, it goes to a vehicle graveyard, also known as the auto salvage yard. If you live in a large city, there are probably more than a few salvage yards to choose from. So when you need a replacement part for your vehicle, try the salvage yards first. (After all, just because a vehicle is no longer on the road doesn't mean it is completely useless.) Before heading out the door, call around first. Most salvage yards have an electronic inventory of their vehicles and can tell you over the phone if they have the same make and model vehicle, whether the part is available, and the price of the part. Most places will pull the part out of the vehicle for you for a fee, or you can pull the part yourself. Obtaining a replacement part from a salvage yard can save you hundreds of dollars and save the energy that would have been required to produce the new product.

If you have no luck finding the vehicle part you need at a salvage yard near you, you can probably purchase a refurbished part from a local auto parts store. A refurbished part will work just as well as a new part and usually comes with a warranty. The store will require a deposit or core charge until they receive the used part from your vehicle, which will be refurbished and sold again. It's like a recycling program for vehicle parts.

78. CONSIDER HYBRID, HYDROGEN FUEL-CELL, ELECTRIC, NATURAL GAS, ETHANOL, AND BIODIESEL CARS

Before purchasing your next vehicle, consider your options. Currently, there are many vehicles to choose from that have vastly improved fuel efficiency over conventional vehicles. Hybrids are becoming very popular as gas prices continue to rise and more people become informed about climate change. Hybrids produce either very low or zero emissions. Many hybrid vehicles are now available from a variety of manufacturers. Hybrid vehicles get better gas mileage because they use an internal battery to power the vehicle in addition to regular gas or diesel.

Although hydrogen-fuel-cell powered vehicles can be very efficient and emit water rather than pollution, we do not currently have the infrastructure to support these cars for everyone. A limited number of hydrogen vehicles will be sold to some California residents in 2008, but most manufacturers are still in the concept phase of development.

Electric vehicles may very well be the best option, since they can be powered solely by electricity and produce no emissions. If you use renewable energy for electricity, operating an electric vehicle would produce no greenhouse gas emissions. Some electric vehicles are now available for purchase, but they are prohibitively expensive. Hopefully, technological advances will reduce the price in the near future.

Ethanol is a renewable fuel produced from corn and other crops. At low levels, ethanol can be mixed with regular gasoline and used in traditional vehicles without special modifications. (You may have noticed a sign at some gasoline pumps stating that the gas contains 10% ethanol.) Flex fuel vehicles (FFVs) can operate on fuel with a higher ratio of ethanol to gas, or they can operate on regular gas. Ethanol burns clean, and using it helps reduce our reliance on foreign oil.

Biodiesel is a renewable fuel made primarily from vegetable or animal oil. For instance, you can save the oil from a deep fryer and use it as fuel. Of course, the oil must undergo some processing before you actually put it in your vehicle. Biodiesel is becoming more popular and is already available at some gas stations for about the same price as a gallon of diesel. Already, many people in South American countries are relying on biodiesel to operate their vehicles. Many older vehicles can be converted to use biodiesel or a mixture of biodiesel and regular diesel. Conversion eliminates the need to buy a new vehicle or to replace vehicles already on the road. This is favorable, as the production of cars is more destructive of the environment than what

they do once we start commuting in them.[26] Biodiesel may be the way to go if you want to reduce your vehicle's emissions or want to get the most out of that old diesel truck you have been hanging on to for years.

Vehicles powered by natural gas, also called NGV, are fuel efficient, significantly cheaper to operate than petroleum-gas vehicles, and less harmful to the environment. In many places in the U.S., you can fill your NGV's tank in about the same amount of time it would take to fill the tank with a regular petroleum-gas pump. Also, you can use the existing natural gas lines from your home and install your own natural gas pump, but filling your car's gas tank will take several hours. According to the U.S. Department of Energy, when compared to conventional gas and diesel vehicles, natural-gas-powered vehicles can reduce carbon dioxide emissions by 25%, nitrogen oxide emissions by 35% to 60%, and other hydrocarbon emissions by 50% to 75%.[27] Because natural gas burns clean, there is less wear and tear on the vehicle, which translates to less repairs and a lower maintenance cost. However, natural gas is a fossil fuel, not a renewable resource, which means that it is a good alternative now but probably not a long-term solution.

Each individual who drives an alternative-fuel car makes a difference. No matter which alternative fuel you decide to use to power your vehicle, you greatly reduce your individual impact on the climate and the air quality. You also support the market for alternative fuels. The more people buying alternative fuels, the more producers we will gain in the marketplace. Furthermore, a high demand and many suppliers means that the average price of all alternative fuels will decrease.

One person flying in an airplane
for one hour is responsible
for the same greenhouse
gas emissions as a typical
Bangladeshi in a whole year.

Beatrice Schell[28]

Travel and Commuting Alternatives

79. RIDE A BICYCLE

Last summer, I worked in New Hampshire for an organization called Clean Air–Cool Planet. I didn't have a vehicle and used only a bicycle to get around all summer. Every morning at work I had to stand in front of the fan in the office for a few minutes to dry off, but I started my day feeling good both mentally and physically. And on my days off, I noticed a feeling of extra energy and realized that my body was telling me to get out on my bike again.

One morning I got dressed in some white dress pants and a nice shirt and headed off to work, riding my bike. It was overcast, but I had been fortunate enough to beat the rain every morning thus far, so I continued on. Suddenly the rain came down hard, so I took shelter under an awning. After waiting about ten minutes, I got impatient and decided to head to work even though it was still raining. I assumed the rain would stop soon, but it didn't. My bike splashed through puddles, and the front tire flicked mud onto my face. After a twenty-minute ride, I made it to work at last. I parked my bike in the parking garage and looked down at my clothes to see the damage. Not only were my clothes splattered with mud, but my white pants were so saturated with water that they were completely see-through. It was Monday, so I knew all of my coworkers would be gathered around for the morning meeting. Luckily, I'd brought some spare clothes in my backpack. As I walked to the building, I wished I hadn't worn red underwear and hoped no one would see me! If only I didn't have to get the key to the bathroom from inside the office, no one would have been the wiser. The point of my story? Although biking can be an enjoyable way to commute to work, I would recommend bringing an extra set of clothing with you, just in case.

So, dust your bike off and give it a spin. If you don't have a bike, you can probably purchase a used one for less than it costs to fill your car's tank with gasoline. Some universities offer bikes for students to rent, free of charge. Biking is a great way to stay fit, commute, and enjoy some fresh air. Give it a try; you might have forgotten how much you enjoy riding a bike.

80. WALK

As comedian Steven Wright once said, "Everywhere is walking distance if you have the time."[29] If you are headed somewhere within a couple miles of your home, consider walking. If distance allows, walk to school with your kids, and to the grocery store, to church, and to friends' houses. When you walk, you don't have to worry about finding a parking space, and the only fuel you burn is calories. People typically walk more if they live in an urban area, and in those areas, you will notice that not as many people are overweight. Walking is also a great way to release endorphins, which makes you feel good. Many people walk for pleasure as well as exercise. By walking to work or to run errands, you're not only saving gas by not using a vehicle, you're also gaining peace of mind. If it's raining, bring an umbrella, and if it's cold outside, bundle up. Take a friend or a pet on your walk and you'll both enjoy it, or maybe you'll meet some new friends in your neighborhood. If walking is too slow for you, use rollerblades, a skateboard, or a scooter to quicken your pace.

81. USE PUBLIC TRANSPORTATION

Public transportation includes buses, light rail, trolleys, commuter trains, cable cars, ferries, vanpool services, monorails, and tramways. Let someone else drive you to work so you can catch up on some sleep, read the paper, make a phone call, or even meet new people. Relax and enjoy the ride instead of arriving at work or home stressed out from driving in traffic. Simplify your life and take back some time for yourself.

Check with your workplace to see if they provide discounted metro and bus passes, or if they will subsidize some of your public transportation or vanpool expenses. And in case you didn't know, federal law allows workers up to $115 each month for commuting expenses related to using public transportation, tax-free! This means you could have up to $115 deducted from your paycheck every month before taxes are calculated, for a total of $1,380 per year, tax-free. If your employer pays for some of your public transportation expenses for commuting to work, they can also receive the same tax benefit. If your workplace doesn't participate in this program, perhaps you should suggest it. Besides, subsidizing public transportation is usually much less expensive than providing parking for employees. Call your local transit authority for more information.

Using public transportation instead of your own vehicle saves you a lot of money and improves the air quality in your community by reducing traffic congestion and the resulting emissions. According to a study from SAIC, switching from driving to using public transportation reduces a person's carbon footprint by about twenty pounds of carbon dioxide per day, which adds up to about 4,800 pounds per year.[30]

82. RIDE AN ELECTRIC MOTORCYCLE OR SCOOTER

Did you know that the carpool lane is also available for motorcycles? That's because motorcycles get excellent gas mileage compared to cars. However, gasoline-powered motorcycles still produce greenhouse gas emissions. If you ride an electric motorcycle or scooter, there are zero emissions. Of course, you shouldn't take a scooter on the freeway because it's illegal, but using an electric scooter for running around town is a much better option than a gas-and-oil-guzzling vehicle.

Some electric motorcycles can run up to sixty-eight miles on a single charge, which is probably less than you drive in a day anyway. If you're commuting more than sixty-eight miles per day, maybe you should consider moving closer to work or taking public transportation. Most electric motorcycles and scooters can be charged using a standard electrical outlet. The price of electricity is about one-tenth that of gasoline, and you can purchase renewable energy from the grid to charge your motorcycle or scooter. An electric motorcycle or scooter is eligible for government rebates and local subsidies, and sometimes tax exemptions are available. So if you can't ride a bicycle or walk, do the next best thing: get an electric motorcycle or scooter.

83. AVOID TRAVELING BY AIRPLANE

Henry David Thoreau once said, "Thank God men cannot fly, and lay waste the sky as well as the earth."[31] Unfortunately, flying has become a common part of many people's lives. If you travel by airplane, it probably makes up the largest segment of your carbon footprint. Since airplanes travel at a high altitude, the emissions from the burning jet fuel have a more harmful effect on the climate than if the same emissions were at ground level. The IPCC estimates that the climate impact from airplanes is two to four times the effect of their emissions alone. If you fly from coast to coast in the United States, the airplane produces two to three tons of emissions per passenger. If you fly to Europe from the east coast of the U.S., the plane produces three to four tons of emissions per passenger. This means that just one trip could account for a quarter to half of your annual carbon footprint! Also, just one trip on a plane could equate to the annual amount of GHG emissions from your vehicle. If you are a frequent flyer, imagine how each trip compounds your carbon footprint.

Avoiding a trip on an airplane could be the easiest and most significant way to reduce your carbon footprint. Instead of flying your family somewhere for your next vacation, explore an area nearby using your vehicle or by taking a train. You may be amazed at what you can enjoy in your own backyard, and you can make the journey part of the adventure. When I was a kid, my parents would pack all six of us into the station wagon to visit relatives in California. We still talk about the memories from those road trips, and I remember the journey more than the actual visit.

If you travel for business, try using video or phone conferencing instead of flying, in order to save time and money. But if you must travel, consider taking a bus or train, especially if you're traveling alone. Stay in touch with family and friends by using web cameras and microphones. When I worked in Australia, seeing and hearing the voices of my family meant the world to me and eased my homesickness.

If you must travel by airplane, produce fewer emissions by minimizing the number of connecting flights and taking the most direct flights possible. Combine business with pleasure and visit friends or family in the area so you don't need to take another flight to the same destination. Pack lighter, since more weight burns more fuel. If you decide to purchase carbon offsets for the GHG emissions produced by your flight, be sure to send your money to an organization certified by the Gold

Standard. See www.cdmgoldstandard.org for more information on gold-standard-certified offsets.

84. EXPLORE YOUR OWN BACKYARD

When planning your next vacation, instead of traveling far away, stay close to home and discover what your own state or region has to offer. I've lived in one state for most of my life, and I'm still discovering beautiful places to spend my free time. I especially enjoy visiting state and national parks; I can still have a new experience every time I visit by doing something different, like biking, hiking, climbing, camping, or canyoneering. Even going somewhere in a different season, such as visiting the desert in the winter, can be a new and beautiful trip. A couple of my friends spent their honeymoon in the same city where they live, but they acted like tourists for the week. They stayed in a very nice hotel downtown and visited all the typical attractions that tourists would enjoy that locals typically take for granted. They said they had a wonderful time, and I was impressed with the originality of the idea.

Spending your vacations near your home means you won't be creating large amounts of emissions traveling by airplane or traveling long distances by car, and the money you spend can help the local economy. For vacation ideas, ask friends and neighbors their favorite local destinations. Invite friends to join you on vacation, and carpool or caravan, depending on the number of people. How much we enjoy a vacation is usually determined by the people we are with rather than where we go.

85. LIVE NEAR YOUR WORKPLACE

Paul Dudley White said, "A vigorous five-mile walk will do more good for an unhappy but otherwise healthy adult than all the medicine and psychology in the world."[32] Even if you don't commute to work every day, living in a community close to where you work, with a nearby grocery store and other essentials, will diminish the amount of time you spend driving your vehicle. If you can walk to work and

the grocery store, you'll save money on gas or other transportation expenses and reduce your carbon footprint as well. Even if you have to spend more money for housing to live closer to your workplace, compare it to the savings from not paying for transportation and you may still come out ahead. Living close to places you go every day could mean that you no longer need to own a

car or that you can reduce the number of cars in your household. You could also enjoy the convenience of running home for lunch during the day instead of eating out. Just imagine how much stress you could alleviate from your life by not dealing with traffic on your way to and from work.

86. SHARE A CAB

If you need to take a cab to travel to a location you can't reach using public transportation, share the cab ride with at least one other person. It's just like carpooling, and you can split the fare as well. There are online services, such as www.rideamigos.com, that can help connect you with someone with which to share a cab. Talk to your neighbors, coworkers, and friends to coordinate sharing taxis on a regular basis instead of riding alone. If you typically use a taxi to commute to work, this can be a great way to carpool on a daily basis and split your cab expenses. If you are visiting a new area, sharing a cab ride can be a better option than renting a car, since it is usually less expensive.

87. RECREATE WITHOUT A MOTOR

Dirt bikes, 4-wheelers (ATVs or quads), snowmobiles, wave-runners, jet-skis, and motorboats are popular recreational vehicles. You've probably headed outdoors at least once to get some fresh air and instead inhaled some of the exhaust from one of these machines. Motorized recreational vehicles burn fossil fuels and cause GHG emissions.

Instead of burning gasoline on a beautiful day, burn calories instead. Try a new recreational activity or enjoy a favorite sport that doesn't require gasoline, such as kayaking, canoeing, snowshoeing, hiking, Nordic skiing, mountain biking, or trail running. You can still enjoy the pleasures of being on the water, hiking in the mountains, and playing in the snow without causing excess emissions. The only thing you'll have to worry about running out of gas is you!

88. ENGAGE IN ECOTOURISM

Even though we can enjoy local vacations, sometimes people are motivated to see different parts of the world for cultural or ecological reasons. Ecotourism follows the principles of traveling in a sustainable manner, including being energy efficient, conserving water, minimizing waste, and supporting economic development of the local communities you visit. Typically ecotourism is nature-based tourism that takes place in areas characterized by special environmental or cultural attractions. Overall, the goal is to have minimal or no impact on the environment and to preserve the cultural diversity of the area. Basically, it is the notion of not only being a conscious, responsible, sustainable traveler, but also protecting and preserving the area for future generations.

Ecotourism is especially important in developing countries where economic pressures are causing the destruction of forests and marine habitats. By visiting areas for their specific ecological attributes, we raise awareness and appreciation for the attraction, and the money spent in the local community supports the preservation of these areas. However, overdevelopment of hotels or resorts and an unlimited number of visitors can be counterproductive. There are many guide and travel services that can help you plan an ecotourism vacation, but be sure to research the organization. The agency or organization should support conservation, nature-based employment, and alternative income for the local community over the obliteration of ecosystems for hunting, agriculture, and logging.

We cannot live for ourselves
alone. Our lives are connected
by a thousand invisible threads,
and along these sympathetic
fibers, our actions run as causes
and return to us as results.[33]

Herman Melville

COMMUNITY INVOLVEMENT

If you have incorporated the suggestions from this book into your lifestyle, you have significantly reduced your own carbon footprint. Now that you have learned how easy it is to save energy and money, it is time to educate and motivate others to follow suit. Being a steward of the environment is important, because future generations are counting on us to deliver the planet to them better than we received it. We all need to work together to allow future generations to have the same privileges this planet has afforded us.

Being active in your community doesn't mean you have to chain yourself to trees or go door to door collecting money from your neighbors, although those activities can serve a purpose. Of course, the more active you are, the greater the results you will achieve, but every effort is important. You may be unsure how active you are willing to be, but you'll never know how rewarding community involvement can be until you try.

Never doubt that a small group of thoughtful, committed citizens can change the world. Indeed, it is the only thing that ever has.[34]

Margaret Mead

In Your "Neighborhood"

89. EDUCATE YOURSELF, THEN EDUCATE OTHERS

Educate yourself before educating others. Obviously, if you are reading this book you are concerned about climate change and want to do your part to solve the problem. It is important to be informed about the science behind climate change and what some of the possible outcomes could be if we continue with business as usual. Personal research is a wonderful way to get answers to your questions from reliable resources. Although the internet is a great resource, make sure that the information you use can be trusted. Anyone can publish material online, so you can't believe everything that you read. Fortunately, it is quite simple to access articles from science journals, as well as information from government studies and reputable organizations.

As you incorporate the principles from this book and other sources, people will probably notice a difference in your daily habits and routines and ask you why. This will present a perfect opportunity for you to discuss what you are doing to lessen the effects of climate change. Many people have been misinformed about climate change, and the only way to open their minds is to discuss their apprehensions. Explain how you formed your understanding based on facts, and share the facts that made an impact on you. Recommend the resources that broadened your knowledge of climate change. It is much harder to disprove climate change than it is to prove it, and we leave the proving to the climate scientists and the opinions to the politicians. You might recommend the IPCC or the Union of Concerned Scientists as a good source of information. Education is the most important way to motivate people to reduce their carbon footprints, so educate your children, your family, and your friends about how they can do so. The more people acting toward a solution, the better chance we have at mitigating the effects of climate change.

90. START A GRASSROOTS CAMPAIGN

The keys to any grassroots campaign are good organization practices and specific goals. Perhaps you want to raise awareness in your community about climate change or want to support a specific change in legislation for your community. Put the problem and solution in writing, especially if your group wants to confront the local government. Then choose one representative to be the spokesperson for the group. Choose a slogan that appeals to your community and will motivate people to act. Establish the campaign by first creating an initial list of supporters, including contact information and

availability. Then raise some seed money to create the official organization. Develop support from community members by making telephone calls, doing door-to-door canvassing, and organizing table displays in public places to educate the community, recruit supporters, obtain signatures on petitions, and solicit donations. Also, create persuasive literature that identifies the issue, motivates people to act, and details the actions they need to take. Be sure the voice of the organization is heard at public meetings, and hold meetings specifically for your group. Getting citizens involved in the public planning process is one of the most effective ways to make an impact on your community. Even though we do not currently have a national policy to limit greenhouse gas emissions, many communities and states have enacted legislation to reduce their impact on the climate.

91. ENCOURAGE YOUR COWORKERS

Hopefully, you are already an example of practicing energy efficiency at work, but why not extend your knowledge to improving the overall energy efficiency of your workplace? Make suggestions and even present your ideas in a formal business proposal to the people in charge. Energy efficiency translates into saving money and improving the bottom line. Since every business seeks to maximize profit, your suggestions will not only reduce emissions caused by your place of work, it will save the company money, which may even lead to a raise for you. Besides encouraging energy efficiency, you can also promote carpooling and using public transportation by proposing incentives for coworkers. Perhaps people that carpool should get the best parking spaces. Or you could organize a program where everyone is encouraged to ride his or her bicycle to work on a certain day of the week, or seek to provide an extra incentive for those that ride a bicycle to work every day. You might even form a climate-conscious committee to continually implement ways for the business and its employees to reduce their carbon footprints. The possibilities are endless, whether it is a large multinational corporation or a small, family-operated business, so get involved at work and you will find each day more fulfilling.

92. PARTICIPATE IN A COMMUNITY GARDEN

Whether you live in a rural or an urban area, a community garden is a wonderful way to build your community, with the added benefit of providing you and your family with fresh vegetables and herbs. Sometimes a family garden will produce more food than the family can consume, whereas a community garden can produce enough food for the entire neighborhood without letting anything go to waste. If there is extra food, it can be donated to local homeless shelters or other humanitarian venues. In urban areas, a community garden is usually planted in an empty lot and can transform a barren area into a beautiful haven. Everyone shares the responsibilities of caring for the garden as well as the rewards. Working together is an excellent way to connect with your neighbors and improve the quality of your life.

Not only can community gardens produce organic food, they can also conserve resources and reduce city heat caused by asphalt streets and parking lots. If you obtain most of your produce from a community garden, you will be eating produce in season that didn't have to travel much further than a few blocks. The produce will be fresher, taste better, and won't require burning fossil fuels to reach you.

93. SUPPORT CITY CLIMATE PROTECTION

Since the United States federal government refused to ratify the international Kyoto Protocol, it is necessary to push for the enactment of climate policy at the state and city level. The Kyoto Protocol set a target for the United States to reduce emissions by 7% by the year 2012, based on emissions levels from 1990. The U.S. Conference of Mayors launched the Mayors Climate Protection Agreement in an effort to adhere to the Kyoto Protocol standards in each city. Currently, over eight hundred mayors across the country have committed their cities to meet or beat the

targets of the Kyoto Protocol, to support the state and federal government to enact policies to reduce GHG emissions as suggested by the Kyoto Protocol, and lastly, to support the U.S. Congress in enacting a national emissions trading system. If your city is not currently participating, get involved and petition your mayor to join the U.S. Mayors Climate Protection Agreement. For a current list of cities that are participating in this program, visit http://usmayors.org/climateprotection/ClimateChange.asp.

94. VOLUNTEER

Volunteering your time and energy to established campaign groups and organizations aimed at creating awareness and initiating solutions to climate change is a beneficial way to make an impact in your local community. Investigate local opportunities that support your views of citizen stewardship and environmental protection. There is a diverse range of volunteer opportunities that can utilize your existing expertise and skills, and even help you learn some new skills. You could volunteer with a friend or involve your entire family.

Even though you will not receive monetary compensation, volunteering is very rewarding. Volunteering is a great way to meet people in your community, learn new skills, strengthen your resumé, raise awareness, network, and gain a sense of fulfillment and accomplishment. If you don't have time to volunteer weekly, plan to volunteer for special events. Even though you may not be at the forefront of the organization, everything you do will contribute to the overall cause and therefore make a difference in your community.

95. SPEAK UP

When I broached the subject of climate change with my family, the discussion quickly escalated into a shouting match, with each person trying to talk louder than the other and no one listening to anyone. When I challenged them about what they believed, no one could tell me where they got the information, and it became more about opinions and feelings than about facts. This type of elevated debate can be very counterproductive, and shouting back is not the way to inform friends and family. However, the heated discussion at least got my family members to question their opinions and do a little more research on their own. I was surprised by their response in the aftermath of the discussion. They became intrigued and started asking me more questions about climate change. The minds of most of my family members were finally opened to what scientists have been saying for years. Without bringing the topic to the table, I would not have known that my own family members were misinformed.

Don't assume that your friends, family, and coworkers are informed about climate change. Take every opportunity to discuss climate change, explain why the issue is important to you, and describe what others can do to make a difference as well as where they can find more information. Providing specific information about how climate change will impact your local environment can encourage members of your community to make personal changes and support efforts to mitigate climate change. Make your voice heard about climate change and inform coworkers, politicians, educators, children, friends, and even casual acquaintances about what each of us can do to reduce our impact on the climate.

96. GET INVOLVED WITH LOCAL ENERGY COMMITTEES

Mitigating climate change involves planning and implementing ways to reduce the level of greenhouse gas emissions in the atmosphere. Reducing the production of greenhouse gas emissions can involve implementing more renewable and sustainable energy sources. Mitigation strategies not only benefit future generations, they can also make immediate positive impacts on your community, such as cleaner air and less pollution. This can lead to an improvement in local public health and even making positive impacts on the local economy. One community in Utah implemented its own wind farm capable of generating enough energy to power the entire city. The strategy for your community needs to be specific to the location and resources available in your area. Forming an energy committee for your city or area is an excellent way to become involved in municipal planning. Clean Air–Cool Planet, a nonprofit organization, developed a community toolkit to inform and support community programs. The toolkit is available online at http://www.cleanair-coolplanet.org/for_communities/toolkit_home.php.

For more information about forming a local energy committee and developing local strategies, visit http://www.cleanair-coolplanet.org/for_communities/energyguide.php.

97. WORK WITH EXISTING ORGANIZATIONS

You are probably already affiliated with a local organization such as a college or university, a church group, a book club, the PTA, or Scouts. Get involved at your children's school and your church and any other organizations to which you belong. Volunteer to invite local speakers and organize events for students and community members to become informed about climate change. Open forums provide an opportunity for questions and teach others how to make a difference.

Begin a strategy for reducing the carbon footprint of the organization. Determining the carbon footprint of an organization requires a more complex calculator than the one you used to calculate your personal carbon footprint. For large organizations like schools and universities, Clean Air–Cool Planet provides a toolkit and a campus carbon calculator that can be downloaded free of charge from their website at http://www.cleanair-coolplanet.org/toolkit/content/view/43/124/. The World Resources Institute (WRI) offers a guide and calculator that can be used for businesses or adapted to your organization. It is available at http://www.wri.org/publication/working-9-5-climate-change-office-guide.

After determining the current emissions level, set goals for the organization to meet by certain deadlines. Get everyone interested and involved in the project—the more people working on the project, the better. Once people have a better understanding of climate change and know how to make an impact, they will probably start making changes in their own life to reduce their carbon footprint.

Knowing is not enough;
we must apply![35]

Goethe

Personal and Political Activism

98. VOTE

Currently the United States does not have a national policy in place to regulate greenhouse gas emissions. It is imperative for our nation to implement sound climate policy, and each year that we delay makes our mitigation response more difficult to implement. Make sure that when you vote for a government official, the candidate understands the issue of climate change and is motivated to enact legislation to regulate emissions. Climate change is an important issue that crosses party lines and should be part of your representative's agenda. Research the candidate's responses for consistency on how they plan to reduce the devastating effects of climate change. Their strategy should be more proactive than reactive. For instance, they should concentrate on a policy for reducing emissions now instead of focusing only on adaptation strategies. If the candidate has not researched the issue of climate change, he or she will probably disappoint you in office.

What distinguishes our country from most other nations is our right to vote. Don't forsake your right to vote! Voting is an important way to place the right representatives in office that will implement climate policies at the national, state, and local levels. This is a critical time for implementing climate policy, and every vote is important. Represent your values and give the next generation a chance to enjoy the beautiful world you have been privileged to live in.

99. BECOME AN INTERNET ACTIVIST

The electronic age has significantly reduced the time and energy required to be actively involved in politics at a local, state, and national level. You could be just a few clicks away from being politically involved. Internet activism ranges from blogging to organizing to propelling campaigns. Getting updated information can be as easy as reading your email when you sign up for email action alerts. Most organizations simplify the process of sending letters to Congress by creating form letters that can be signed electronically and  sent through email. To track changes and keep up on upcoming climate legislation, regularly check out www.congress.org. The congress.org website can also be used for lobbying members of Congress, elected leaders in the White House, and even state legislators by fax or email. The site can also be used to send out your own action alerts to enlist the help of others. There are many ways to use the internet as an effective tool to get information and to help set climate policy in motion, but always remember to check the source of any information you find online.

100. STAY INFORMED

As science and technology progress, there will always be new ways to reduce your carbon footprint. Stay informed as to the latest technology, and do your research before making any significant purchase. For example, the water heater in our home started leaking and was beyond repair. Before running out to replace the water heater, we checked out our options first. We found a small, wall-mounted water heater that produces hot water instantly instead of heating an entire tank of water. These water heaters are much more energy efficient and save money over time when compared to typical water heaters, even though the small, instant heaters cost quite a bit more up front.

In order to meet the rising demands of energy-conscious consumers, manufacturers are producing more efficient and effective products. Even energy companies are making strides by investing in renewable energy. Know where the products you purchase are coming from and how they can affect the climate. A little research can save you a lot of money in the long run and can significantly reduce your carbon footprint. Supporting new technology that reduces your carbon footprint increases the demand for that product, which decreases the price so that the technology is more widely available for everyone.

101. PASS IT ON

Now that you have finished making one hundred changes in your life, you are off to a great start and have probably drastically reduced your carbon footprint. Continue making a difference by passing this book on to a friend or family member. As you share your experience with him or her, he or she may be motivated to make personal changes. If possible, share what you're learning in this book in daily conversations. Propose this book as the next title for your book club, and discuss the steps you've taken to reduce your own carbon footprint. Donate the book to your local library or give it to someone as a gift. It doesn't matter how you pass on the information, only that you start informing and prompting others to reduce their carbon footprints. Each of us can make a difference! Start the chain reaction that will help our entire nation become climate conscious.

1. Marian Wright Edelman, *Families in Peril: An Agenda for Social Change* (Cambridge, MA: Harvard University Press, 1987).

2. Hale, Edward Everett, "Lend a Hand," in *Masterpieces of Religious Verse,* ed. James Dalton Morrison (1948), 416.

3. John Robins, *The Food Revolution* (Newburyport, MA: Conari Press, 2001).

4. "Overview of U.S. Meat and Poultry Production and Consumption," American Meat Institute, 2003.

5. Pat Franklin, "Down the Drain: Plastic Water Bottles Should No Longer Be a Wasted Resource," *Waste Management World,* May/June 2006 (Container Recycling Institute).

6. *Bottled Water Continues Tradition of Strong Growth in 2005,* Beverage Marketing Corp., Apr. 13, 2006.

7. A. Harden and Karl Flecker, "Student Action: Bottled Water: the Industry, the Marketing, the Ruse," OSSTF Education Forum, May 31, 2007.

8. Rich Pirog and Andrew Benjamin, "Checking the Food Odometer: Comparing Food Miles for Local Versus Conventional Produce Sales in Iowa Institutions," Leopold Center for Sustainable Agriculture (Ames, IA: Iowa State University, July 2003).

9. Ibid.

10. Joanne Veto, "U.S. Postal Service Announces 'Cradle to Cradle' Certification," News Release 07–051, June 2007.

11. Henrik Tikkanen, Finnish author (1924–1984), quoted in Larry Chang, *Wisdom for the Soul: Five Millennia of Prescriptions for Spiritual Healing* (Washington, DC: Gnosophia Publishers, 2006).

12. Franklin, Benjamin, *Autobiography of Benjamin Franklin* (New York: Garden City Publishing, 1916), 334.

13. "Refrigerator Energy Use Data," www.waptac.org (website of the Weatherization Assistance Program Technical Assistance Center). Energy use data for over 41,000 refrigerators, refrigerator-freezers, and freezers was compiled by D&R International, Ltd., for the Department of Energy, using the *Directory of Certified Refrigerators, Freezers, and Refrigerator Freezers,* published by the

California Energy Commission (CEC) from 1979 to 1992, except for the year 1991, for which no directory is available (http://www.waptac.org/sp.asp?mc=techaids_refrigerator_energy use).

14. "Refrigerators and Freezers: Residential Refrigerators," U.S. Environmental Protection Agency, U.S. Department of Energy (http://www.energystar.gov/index.cfm?c=refrig.pr_refrigerators).

15. Rebecca Smith, "That Giant Sucking Sound May Be Your New TV: Flat-Panel Displays Devour Power, Even Before Add-Ons; Energy Star Blurs the Picture," *The Wall Street Journal*, Dec. 13, 2007.

16. Neil Postman, "Influence of Television" (http://realitytunnel.com/TV%20and%20the%20%20 mind%20of%20the%20public.htm).

17. Jamie Poolos, *Ralph Waldo Emerson: The Father of the American Renaissance* (New York: The Rosen Publishing Group, 2006), 75.

18. Project Laundry List (www.laundrylist.org).

19. "Energy Saver: Tips on Saving Energy and Money at Home," U.S. Department of Energy: Energy Efficiency and Renewable Energy (http://www1.eere.energy.gov/consumer/tips/laundry.html).

20. Ibid.

21. *Appliance Wise Guide*, National Grid, 2000 (http://www.nationalgridus.com/non_html/shared_ energyeff.pdf).

22. President Lyndon B. Johnson, upon signing the Wilderness Act of 1964 (www.theparksco.com/ explore/park_quotes_cont.html).

23. "Patio heaters produce more CO_2 than a small city," Green Building Press (http://www. newbuilder.co.uk/news/NewsFullStory.asp?ID=2020).

24. Bill Strickland, *The Quotable Cyclist: Great Moments of Bicycling Wisdom, Inspiration and Humor* (Halcottsville, NY: Breakaway Books, 1997), 16.

25. Paul MacCready, U.S. inventor of innovative flying machines, quoted in Cutler J. Cleveland, Christopher G. Morris, and Chris Morris, *Dictionary of Energy* (2005), 501.

26. Chris Balish, *How to Live Well Without Owning a Car: Save Money, Breathe Easier, and Get More Mileage out of Life* (Newburyport, MA: Ten Speed Press, 2006).

27. "Natural Gas Vehicle Emissions," U.S. Department of Energy: Energy Efficiency and Renewable Energy (http://www.eere.energy.gov/afdc/vehicles/natural_gas_emissions.html).

28. Beatrice Schell, "Climate Change," *New Scientist,* Sept. 2006 (http://environment.newscientist.com/channel/earth/climate-change/dn9911-quotes-climate-change.html).

29. Dreyer, Danny, and Katherine Dreyer, *Chi Walking: The Five Mindful Steps for Lifelong Health and Energy* (New York: Simon and Schuster, 2006), 219.

30. Todd Davis and Monica Hale, "Public Transportation's Contribution to Greenhouse Gas Reduction," Science Applications International Corporation (SAIC), 2007.

31. Henry David Thoreau, *The Writings of Henry David Thoreau* (Boston: Houghton Mifflin, 1887), 110.

32. Phillips, Bob, *Phillips' Book of Great Thoughts, Funny Sayings* (Carol Stream, IL: Tyndale House Publishers, Inc., 1993), 211.

33. John Cook, Steve Deger, and Leslie Ann Gibson, *The Book of Positive Quotations* (Minneapolis: Fairview Press, 2007), 101.

34. Margaret Mead, *The World Ahead: An Anthropologist Anticipates the Future* (New York: Berghahn Books, 2005), 12.

35. Nicholas Boyle, *Goethe: The Poet and the Age* (2000), 484.

Index